Qur'an's
Prescription for Life
Revealed Cosmic Maps and Prescriptions

Distributed & Published by Zahra Publications
PO Box 50764
Wierda Park 0149
Centurion
South Africa
E-mail: zp@sfhfoundation.com
www.sfhfoundation.com

© 2015 Shaykh Fadhlalla Haeri

All rights reserved. Except for brief quotations in critical articles or reviews, no part of this book may be reproduced or utilised in any form or by any means, electronic or mechanical, without permission in writing from the publisher.

Design & Typeset in South Africa by Mizpah Marketing Concepts
Cover Design by Mizpah Marketing Concepts

To Purchase an ebook version of this book, please visit the eBook portal on http://www.sfhfoundation.com/books.html or www.zahrapublications.com

ISBN: 978-1-919826-90-5

CONTENTS

Acknowledgements		5
Introduction		7
Chapter 1	Qur'an	13
Chapter 2	Allah	21
Chapter 3	Allah's Ways	29
Chapter 4	Allah's Commands	49
Chapter 5	Allah's Prohibitions	59
Chapter 6	Allah's Creation	67
Chapter 7	Prophets and Messengers	81
Chapter 8	The Religion (*Dīn*)	97
	a. Living Islam, faith (*imān*), excellence (*ihsān*)	99
	b. Correct Transactions	107
	c. Supplications	112
Chapter 9	The Adamic Self	117
Chapter 10	Nations and Cultures	131
Chapter 11	Believers (*Mu'minūn*)	143
Chapter 12	Unbelievers (*Kāfirūn*)	155
Chapter 13	The Hereafter (*Ākhirah*)	165
Conclusion		175

ACKNOWLEDGEMENTS

This book first appeared about 25 years ago and was reprinted 5 times over the years. Several friends, associates and family members had helped in its evolvement and appearance in the present form. These people were remembered in previous editions. The present version owes its appearance to Abbas and Muna Bilgrami and Leyya Kalla with the back up and support of Musab Al Khateeb, Hashim Ismail and Yunus Ismail.

BISMILLAH AL WAHID AL AHAD

INTRODUCTION

The Qur'an means that which is to be read, or that which has been gathered, the known and the unknown. It connects and relates minute and mundane aspects of creation to the most subtle and divine realities. The Qur'an is the foundation of the religion (*dīn*)[1], containing as it does Allah's ways, patterns, purpose and direction of creation. The way of the Prophet Muhammad (peace and blessings be upon him)[2] completes the *dīn*.

Through the Qur'an Allah reveals to us His unique Oneness and His Attributes. All facets of the knowledge of unity in creation, prophethood, the return to Allah, resurrection, heaven and hell, personal and social directives, and commands and prohibitions – all originate from the Qur'an. Furthermore it records for us many stories of the prophets and other beings with relevance to the path. The Qur'an lays the foundation of Islamic jurisprudence, which was elaborated and completed by the prophetic way (*sunnah*). From the early days, Muslims based their conduct on the Qur'an and the prophetic pattern of life. Throughout the centuries elaborate and diverse commentaries on the Qur'an have been produced, and much has been narrated regarding prophecies and miracles related in the Qur'an.

---

1 *Dīn* has a meaning, which is distinctly different from religion. The meaning is more akin to total life transaction. The true Muslim sees no separation between his *dīn* and his life. Islam is not a religion practised separately from life.

2 It is customary to invoke peace and blessings on the Prophet whenever his name is mentioned.

The Qur'an as it appears in the actual book form, which we read today, was perfected so as to preserve its pristine message. Originally the Qur'an was written in the 'kufic' script without vowelization marks. Vowelization was perfected almost two centuries after the Prophet's migration (*hijra*) to Medina (circa 9th century Gregorian calendar). Later on numbers were inserted at the end of each verse (*āyah*) and additional embellishments were added, such as division into thirty parts (*juz'*), and further subdivisions of each juz' into quarters (*hizb*), and markings and points of correct pronunciation (*tajwīd*), all in an effort to render the Qur'an more easily memorizable and to beautify recitation. The Qur'an first became available in print 150 years ago, and by the early 20th century printed editions had become widely popularized. Millions of beautifully printed copies of the Qur'an and dozens of translations are readily available today.

The purpose of this collection is to highlight key issues revealed in the Qur'an and to make these gems accessible and usable, with easy reference to key issues concerning life and the path of Islam. When the verses (*āyāt*) are gathered according to topic a clear and more comprehensive picture emerges, enabling us to contemplate these topics more easily and in greater detail. An arrangement of verses as presented in this work emphasizes the vital and transformative teachings of the *dīn*. By hearing or knowing the truth and acting upon it, transformation and awakening take place.

Until the early 20th century numerous Muslim communities in Asia, Africa and Europe lived in accordance with Islamic teachings in cultures and societies reflecting simple variations of the original Muslim communities. With the advent of Western material dominance and the fragmentation of the world of Islam along ethnic, national and geo-political lines, the old preserved Muslim enclaves began to erode and were replaced with rituals, ceremonies, nostalgia and sometimes anger and frustration. The path of Islam now needs to be earned by study, reflection, application and absorption.

Most people in our time lack exposure to the true meaning of Islam, which is the ultimate exposition of spiritual knowledge. Many Muslims who assume that their culture or School of Law (*madhhab*) is the only right path to enlightenment also need to be exposed to original Islam directly through the Qur'an and the prophetic example.

Muslims and non-Muslims alike are pressed for time nowadays and suffer from information 'overload' and other modern diseases, and thus need spiritual remedies prepared in a manner that can be acquired and assimilated more readily. With this collection, I hope to help overcome to some extent the lack of time and knowledge of Arabic, as well as the cultural, ethnic or theological barriers to the great Qur'anic fountainhead.

Allah's creation, its purpose and direction, are laid out according to perfect designs and patterns. In order for our innate nature (*fitrah*) to develop in recognizing and adhering to those inherently harmonious ways, we need to grasp the full code of the *dīn*. The Qur'an contains the foundational knowledge of that code. It unveils the way to Allah by Allah's mercy (*rahmah*) and equally identifies the cul-de-sac that draws us into confusion and self-destruction. It describes in detail the character, conduct and path of the believer and also the bleak picture of the non-believer. It highlights the pitfalls of the ego-self (*nafs*) and how one may sublimate and transform into an enlightened being. As well as addressing the individual, the Qur'an also addresses mankind on a social level through the many references to nations being destroyed by their wrong deeds.

The chapters on Allah, His ways, commands and prohibitions contain the most prominent regulatory patterns in natural creation. Everything in existence has been designed perfectly, and human endeavour is needed to uncover and apply the appropriate ways of interacting in the world.

In the chapter on Allah's Creation, more specific general laws and decrees have been highlighted. These laws and decrees were revealed to the prophets and messengers - who were enlightened beings - with appropriate paths of leadership and governance for their time.

The chapter on the *dīn* includes matters of faith and transformative worship as well as appropriate codes of conduct. The prophetic character of Muhammad, may the peace and blessings of Allah be upon him, was the perfect example of living Islam.

The chapter on the Adamic Self reveals the Islamic cosmology of the lower self and how it veils the divine spirit within, whereas nations and cultures amplify the point that following the intended natural way will result in prosperity and development. Denial or distraction from the practice of correct conduct will result in self-destruction.

The chapters on the believers and unbelievers clearly show how two different agendas and ways of life occur side by side in this transient world. The unbelievers are preparing themselves for an eternal hell by creating mini-hells on earth, while the believers are already accessing the bliss of the garden within.

The last chapter on The Hereafter describes how each individual, as well as societies, will come to reap what they have sown in this world. Pure actions, prophetically guided, with spontaneous awareness of the Divine Presence, will result in illumination in this world in preparation for the Hereafter. Waywardness in this world will strengthen veils and obscure the Divine Presence, thus eliminating self-awareness and accountability – a recipe for confusion, disruption, and preparation for hell. Allah reminds us repeatedly in the Qur'an that the believer's responsibility is to perfect his or her worship by sacrifice, submission, inner contentment and constant striving. These are the ingredients of transformation for which every intelligent human being strives.

Human search, struggle and high aspiration for perfection and beauty will continue forever. Experiencing the Garden in this world is only a temporary reflection of paradise in the Hereafter. The *dīn* of Islam, based on the Qur'an and the prophetic way, is the map that will take us from this world of change and uncertainty to the abode of eternal bliss and happiness. This map reveals the boundaries and the direction that will lead us back to our home where Adam and Eve came into being.

This collection was put together in the name of the All-Compassionate Merciful, in order to enable us to recite, know, absorb and live the truth of (*Lā ilāha illā Allāh, Muhammadun Rasūl Allāh*).

Shaykh Fadhlalla Haeri
November 2015 - South Africa

CHAPTER ONE

QUR'AN

The Qur'an is the revealed knowledge and light that encompasses the patterns, meanings and purpose of existence. Throughout the history of mankind, Divine Revelation descended on numerous occasions and several named prophets were known to have received and declared divine books. The final message that compasses all that went before is the Qur'an.

The root of the word 'Qur'an' is derived from the Arabic noun, which originally means 'collection'; *qara'a*, the verbal root, means 'to read' or 'to recite'. The Qur'an in our present day is considered by all accounts to be the most universally read book in the world.

The Qur'an first descended upon the Prophet on the Night of Power (*Laylat al-Qadr*) when he was forty years old, but was revealed gradually over the following 23 years. The specific occasions for the revelation of many of the verses (*āyāt*) has been narrated and recorded by the Prophet's companions and progeny. The chapters that were revealed in Mecca generally address human beings and major creational issues, whereas most of the Madinan chapters relate to the revealed code of personal and social conduct, worship and other social and legal matters.

During the Prophet's lifetime the Qur'an was collected by several of his close companions. The rapid spread of Islam necessitated standardization to eliminate the possibility of corruption of the original text. The third Caliph, Uthman, undertook the task using the Quarayshi dialect. He had the standard distributed to the main centers within the Muslim lands. A few years later the codification of the rules concerning Arabic grammar and orthography was begun by the Caliph 'Ali Ibn Abi Talib. From then on, numerous Islamic scholars have reviewed and excelled in all aspects of study related to the Qur'an, Allah's final and completed revelation.

Qur'anic science covers exegesis or commentary (*tafsir*), its inimitability (*i'jaz*), the historical context in which the verse was revealed (*asbab al-nuzul*), grammar (*nahw*), eloquence (*balaghah*) and readings (*qira'at*). The Qur'an has been also given other names such as the Book (*al-kitab*), the Discrimination (*al-furqan*), the Guidance (*al-huda*), the Remembrance (*al-dhikr*) and others. The Qur'an unfolds the knowledge of Allah's oneness and Attributes, prophethood, the return, the revealed code of conduct, numerous parables, prophecies and sustainable guidelines for personal and social responsibility. Above all it illumines the way to freedom from the desires of mind and body and dispels darkness and ignorance.

There are many levels of understanding the meanings of the Qur'an. The book has common, outer meanings and deep inner meanings, which have within them many layers of subtle knowledge. Imam 'Ali said that every verse in the Qur'an has four facets. One is the outer having to do with recitation and hearing. The second is understanding and comprehension. The third is acquaintance with the boundaries and injunctions relating to what is prohibited and allowed. The fourth is subtle and connects with what Allah desires from His servant and bestows upon him.

The Qur'an contains the blueprint for the perfect manner of transaction with oneself, society and the Creator. It is Divine Essence manifested in a manner that can be absorbed and followed by any human being who seeks transformation and awakening to the everlasting source within the heart. Indeed wherever one looks there is the sign of the Creator. We can only look due to His grace and generosity.

1.

الم
ذَٰلِكَ ٱلْكِتَٰبُ لَا رَيْبَ ۛ فِيهِ ۛ هُدًى لِّلْمُتَّقِينَ
ٱلَّذِينَ يُؤْمِنُونَ بِٱلْغَيْبِ وَيُقِيمُونَ ٱلصَّلَوٰةَ وَمِمَّا رَزَقْنَٰهُمْ يُنفِقُونَ
وَٱلَّذِينَ يُؤْمِنُونَ بِمَا أُنزِلَ إِلَيْكَ وَمَا أُنزِلَ مِن قَبْلِكَ وَبِٱلْءَاخِرَةِ هُمْ يُوقِنُونَ
أُو۟لَٰٓئِكَ عَلَىٰ هُدًى مِّن رَّبِّهِمْ ۖ وَأُو۟لَٰٓئِكَ هُمُ ٱلْمُفْلِحُونَ

Alif Lām Mīm This is the Book; in it there is no doubt. It is guidance for those in awareness (*taqwā*). Those who have faith (*īmān*) in the unseen, establish prayer (*salāt*), and spend of what We have bestowed upon them, And who have faith in that which has been sent down to you and what was sent down before you, and are certain about the Hereafter (*Ākhirah*). They follow guidance from their Lord. They are the successful.

2/1-5

Allah's Book contains the truth. Only those with insight can read and comprehend His Book. They are guided and thus successful.

Faith and belief are founded upon trust in the perfection of Allah's ways and the prophetic path.

2.

إِنَّآ أَنزَلْنَٰهُ فِى لَيْلَةِ ٱلْقَدْرِ
وَمَآ أَدْرَىٰكَ مَا لَيْلَةُ ٱلْقَدْرِ
لَيْلَةُ ٱلْقَدْرِ خَيْرٌ مِّنْ أَلْفِ شَهْرٍ
تَنَزَّلُ ٱلْمَلَٰٓئِكَةُ وَٱلرُّوحُ فِيهَا بِإِذْنِ رَبِّهِم مِّن كُلِّ أَمْرٍ
سَلَٰمٌ هِىَ حَتَّىٰ مَطْلَعِ ٱلْفَجْرِ

Certainly We sent it down on the Night of Power. And what will convey to you what the Night of Power is? The Night of Power is better than a thousand months. The angels and the Spirit descend in it, by the permission of their Lord, with all decrees. Peace it is until the rising of dawn.

97/1-5

Creation occurred through Allah's power and will before time and space. From this realm the original divine command beams forth and angels descend to reveal the Book of creation and the world of duality and plurality.

The Divine Book contains the primal alphabet of all creational realities, the transient world as well as the permanent abode of the Hereafter. Whoever follows His Book will progress and arrive. Those who don't are lost in the cosmic wilderness.

The most precious gift is His Book, which has descended from the most high and subtle to the world of physical creation and sensory experience as a reminder of the ever-present source and essence.

3.

إِنْ هُوَ إِلَّا ذِكْرٌ لِّلْعَالَمِينَ
لِمَن شَاءَ مِنكُمْ أَن يَسْتَقِيمَ

It is nothing but a reminder to the worlds. To those among you who wish to go straight.

81/27-28

4.

ٱلْحَمْدُ لِلَّهِ ٱلَّذِي أَنزَلَ عَلَىٰ عَبْدِهِ ٱلْكِتَٰبَ وَلَمْ يَجْعَل لَّهُۥ عِوَجَا
قَيِّمًا لِّيُنذِرَ بَأْسًا شَدِيدًا مِّن لَّدُنْهُ وَيُبَشِّرَ ٱلْمُؤْمِنِينَ ٱلَّذِينَ يَعْمَلُونَ ٱلصَّٰلِحَٰتِ أَنَّ لَهُمْ أَجْرًا حَسَنًا

Praise belongs to Allah who has sent the Book down to His slave and has not placed in it any deviation. (Guiding) aright, to give warning of severe punishment from Him and to bring to the believers who do good works the news that theirs will be an excellent reward.

18/1-2

5.

إِنَّهُۥ لَقُرْءَانٌ كَرِيمٌ
فِي كِتَٰبٍ مَّكْنُونٍ
لَّا يَمَسُّهُۥ إِلَّا ٱلْمُطَهَّرُونَ
تَنزِيلٌ مِّن رَّبِّ ٱلْعَٰلَمِينَ

It is indeed a noble Qur'an, In a Book (divinely) protected. No one may touch it but the purified. A revelation sent down from the Lord of the Worlds.

56/77-80

6.

لَوْ أَنزَلْنَا هَٰذَا ٱلْقُرْآنَ عَلَىٰ جَبَلٍ لَّرَأَيْتَهُۥ خَٰشِعًا مُّتَصَدِّعًا مِّنْ خَشْيَةِ ٱللَّهِ ۚ وَتِلْكَ ٱلْأَمْثَٰلُ نَضْرِبُهَا لِلنَّاسِ لَعَلَّهُمْ يَتَفَكَّرُونَ
هُوَ ٱللَّهُ ٱلَّذِى لَآ إِلَٰهَ إِلَّا هُوَ ۖ عَٰلِمُ ٱلْغَيْبِ وَٱلشَّهَٰدَةِ ۖ هُوَ ٱلرَّحْمَٰنُ ٱلرَّحِيمُ
هُوَ ٱللَّهُ ٱلَّذِى لَآ إِلَٰهَ إِلَّا هُوَ ٱلْمَلِكُ ٱلْقُدُّوسُ ٱلسَّلَٰمُ ٱلْمُؤْمِنُ ٱلْمُهَيْمِنُ ٱلْعَزِيزُ ٱلْجَبَّارُ ٱلْمُتَكَبِّرُ ۚ سُبْحَٰنَ ٱللَّهِ عَمَّا يُشْرِكُونَ
هُوَ ٱللَّهُ ٱلْخَٰلِقُ ٱلْبَارِئُ ٱلْمُصَوِّرُ ۖ لَهُ ٱلْأَسْمَآءُ ٱلْحُسْنَىٰ ۚ يُسَبِّحُ لَهُۥ مَا فِى ٱلسَّمَٰوَٰتِ وَٱلْأَرْضِ ۖ وَهُوَ ٱلْعَزِيزُ ٱلْحَكِيمُ

If We had caused this Qur'an to descend upon a mountain, you would certainly have seen it humbled, split apart because of the fear of Allah. Such parables have We set forth for mankind so that they may reflect. He is Allāh; there is no God but Him, the knower of the invisible and the visible. He is the Beneficent, the Merciful. He is Allah, there is no God but Him, the King, the Sacred, the Bestower of Peace, the Trustworthy, the Guardian, the Almighty, the Compeller, and the Supremely Great Glorified is Allah from what they associate (with Him). He is Allah, the Creator, the Maker, the Fashioner His are the most beautiful names. All that is in the heavens and earth glorifies Him, and He is the Almighty, the All – Wise.

59/21-24

Allah is He who knows whatever is the seen and unseen. It is He whose glorious Names and Attributes attract and sustain all His worlds.

It is His Essence that permeates all existences. His Supreme Power is beyond human comprehension.

His Book is the Highway Code for guidance and arrival at the Truth. This code encompasses all the levels and facets of manifestation and levels of consciousness.

His book is echoed in the hearts of the sincere seeker. Its light is primal, effulgent, and the source of guidance.

The manifested Qur'an is in the language of the people of the last messenger: Arabic. Its message and mercy are universal, for all people and for all times.

The souls of the prophets and divine beings witness and live this divine truth.

7.

إِنَّا أَنزَلْنَا عَلَيْكَ الْكِتَابَ لِلنَّاسِ بِالْحَقِّ فَمَنِ اهْتَدَىٰ فَلِنَفْسِهِ وَمَن ضَلَّ فَإِنَّمَا يَضِلُّ عَلَيْهَا وَمَا أَنتَ عَلَيْهِم بِوَكِيلٍ

We have sent down to you the book for mankind with truth. Then he who receives guidance benefits his own soul, and he who goes astray does so to his own detriment. And you are not a guardian over them.

39/41

8.

طه
مَا أَنزَلْنَا عَلَيْكَ الْقُرْآنَ لِتَشْقَىٰ
إِلَّا تَذْكِرَةً لِّمَن يَخْشَىٰ
تَنزِيلًا مِّمَّنْ خَلَقَ الْأَرْضَ وَالسَّمَاوَاتِ الْعُلَى

Ta Ha. We have not sent down the Qur'an upon you to cause you distress, but as a reminder to him who has fear. A revelation from Him Who created the earth and the high heavens.

20/1-4

9.

قُرْآنًا عَرَبِيًّا غَيْرَ ذِي عِوَجٍ لَّعَلَّهُمْ يَتَّقُونَ

An Arabic Qur'an with no distortion in it, so that they will be in constant awareness (taqwā).

39/28

10.

وَنَزَّلْنَا عَلَيْكَ الْكِتَابَ تِبْيَانًا لِّكُلِّ شَيْءٍ وَهُدًى وَرَحْمَةً وَبُشْرَىٰ لِلْمُسْلِمِينَ

… We have revealed the Book to you to make everything clear, as guidance and as a mercy, and is good news for all who are in submission (Muslims).

16/89

Qur'an

11.

مَا نَنسَخْ مِنْ ءَايَةٍ أَوْ نُنسِهَا نَأْتِ بِخَيْرٍ مِّنْهَا أَوْ مِثْلِهَا ۗ أَلَمْ تَعْلَمْ أَنَّ اللَّهَ عَلَىٰ كُلِّ شَيْءٍ قَدِيرٌ

Whatever revealed verse *(ayah)* We abrogate or cause to be forgotten, We bring one better than it or its like. Do you not know that Allah has power over all things?

2/106

12.

وَإِذَا قُرِئَ الْقُرْآنُ فَاسْتَمِعُوا لَهُ وَأَنصِتُوا لَعَلَّكُمْ تُرْحَمُونَ

And when the Qur'an is recited, Listen to it and pay heed so that hopefully you gain mercy.

7/204

13.

أَفَلَا يَتَدَبَّرُونَ الْقُرْآنَ ۚ وَلَوْ كَانَ مِنْ عِندِ غَيْرِ اللَّهِ لَوَجَدُوا فِيهِ اخْتِلَافًا كَثِيرًا

Will they not ponder upon the Qur'an? If it had been from other than Allah, they would have found much inconsistency in it.

4/82

14.

قُل لَّئِنِ اجْتَمَعَتِ الْإِنسُ وَالْجِنُّ عَلَىٰ أَن يَأْتُوا بِمِثْلِ هَٰذَا الْقُرْآنِ لَا يَأْتُونَ بِمِثْلِهِ وَلَوْ كَانَ بَعْضُهُمْ لِبَعْضٍ ظَهِيرًا

Say: Truly! If both mankind and the invisible entities *(jinn)* should assemble to produce the like of this Qur'an, they could not produce the like of it, even if they were fully supporting each other.

17/88

His mercy can only be completely understood when we pay attention to the truth and turn away from falsehood. This implies purity of heart, presence of mind, utter sincerity, honesty and yearning for His perfections at all times.

The Truth is constant, consistent, and absolute. Enlightenment is access to it at all times and circumstances. This is the root of guidance and knowledge.

CHAPTER TWO

ALLAH

Allah is the ultimate divine name expressing Absolute Essence from which all Attributes, names and manifestations emanate. The name Allah covers whatever is known and unknown, but cannot be limited by creational indications or attempts.

All great Attributes, which we desire and seek, belong to Allah and yet His Essence is independent of all qualities or descriptions. The most effulgent manifestation of Allah is the Lord (*Rabb*) of all kingdoms, before time and after.

Divine names mentioned in the Qur'an include the following one hundred:

Al-Rabb – The Lord. *Al-Rahmān* – The All-Merciful. *Al-Rahīm* – The All-Compassionate. *Al-Malik* – The King. *Al-Quddūs* - The Most Pure. *Al-Salaam* - The Bestower of Peace. *Al-Mu'min* - The Trustworthy. *Al-Muhaymin* - The Protector. *Al-'Azīz* - The All Mighty. *Al-Jabbār* - The Compeller. *Al-Mutakabbir* - The Supremely Great. *Al-Khāliq* - The Creator. *Al-Bāri'* - The Maker. *Al-Musawwir* - The Fashioner. *Al-Ghaffār* - The Coverer of all Faults. *Al-Qahhar* - The Subduer. *Al-Wahhāb* - The Bestower. *Al-Razzāq* - The Provider. *Al-Fattāh* - The Opener. *Al-'Alīm* - The All-Knowing. *Al-Qābid* - The Restrictor. *Al-Bāsit* - The Expander. *Al-Khāfid* - The One Who Lowers. *Al-Rāfi'* - The Exalter. *Al-Mu'izz* -

The Honourer. *Al-Mudhill* - The Abaser. *Al-Samī'*- The All-Hearing. *Al-Basīr* - The All-Seeing. *Al-Hakam* - The Judge. *Al-'Adl* - The Just. *Al-Latīf* - The Subtle. *Al-Khabīr* - The All-Cognizant. *Al-Halīm* - The Clement. *Al-'Adhim* - The Magnificent. *Al-Ghafūr* - The All-Forgiving. *Al-Shakūr* - The Grateful. *Al-'Alī* - The Most High. *Al-Kabīr* - The Most Great. *Al-Hafīdh* - The Preserver. *Al-Muqīt* - The Sustainer. *Al-Hasīb* - The One who satisfies Needs. *Al-Jalīl* - The Majestic. *Al-Karīm* - The Most Generous. *Al-Raqīb* - The All-Vigilant. *Al-Mujīb* - The Responder. *Al-Wāsi'* - The All-Encompassing. *Al-Hakīm* - The Most Wise. *Al-Wadūd* - The All-Loving. *Al-Majīd* - The Most Glorious. *Al-Bā'ith* - The Resurrector. *Al-Shahīd* – The Witnesser. *Al-Haqq* - The Absolute Truth. *Al-Wakīl* - The Guardian Trustee. *Al-Qawī* - The Most Strong. *Al-Matīn* - The Firm. *Al- Walī* - The Patron. *Al-Hamīd* - The Praiseworthy. *Al-Muhsī* - The Appraiser. *Al-Mubdi'* - The Originator. *Al-Mu'īd* - The Returner. *Al-Muhyī* - The Life-Giver. *Al-Mumīt* - The Death-Giver. *Al-Hayy* - The Ever-Living. *Al-Qayyūm* - The All-Sustaining. *Al-Wājid* – The Manifestor. *Al-Mājid* - The Most Splendid. *Al-Ahad* – The Absolute One. *Al- Samad* - The Self-Sufficient. *Al- Qādir* - The Most Able. *Al-Muqtadir* - The All-Powerful. *Al-Muqaddim* - The Expediter. *Al-Mu'akhkhir* - The Postponer. *Al-Awwal* – The First. *Al- Akhir* - The Last. *Al-Dhāhir* - The Manifest. *Al-Batin* - The Concealed. *Al-Barr* - The Benefactor. *Al-Tawwāb* - The Most Accepting of Repentance. *Al-Muntaqim* - The Avenger. *Al-'Afu* - The Pardoner. *Al-Ra'ūf* - The Most Affectionate. *Malik Al-Mulk* - The Master of The Kingdom. *Dhūl-Jalāli wa al-Ikrām* - The Master of Majesty and Nobility. *Al-Wālī* – The Governor. *Al-Muta'āli* - The Most Exalted. *Al-Muqsit* - The All-Equitable. *Al-Jāmi'* - The Gatherer. *Al-Ghanī* - The Rich Beyond Need. *Al-Mughnī* - The Enricher. *Al-Māni'* - The Preventer. *Al-Darr* - The Bestower of Affliction. *Al-Nafi'* - The Beneficial. *Al-Nūr* - The Light. *Al-Hādī* - The Guide. *Al-Badī* - The Originator. *Al-Bāqī* - The Everlasting. *Al-Wārith* - The Inheritor. *Al-Rashid* - The Most Discerning. *Al-Sabūr* - The Patient. *Al-Wāhid* - The One.

The path of Divine Unity (*Tawhīd*) begins with the intellect searching for the relationship between outer events and causes, between actions and meanings. A subtler realm of unity occurs between Attributes such as the opposites of beauty and majesty, as well as between ease and difficulty, or the outer and the inner. The Ultimate reality of Essence is the One Source behind all actions and attributes, both seen and unseen.

Every human being is driven along the path of unity by the original primal desire for happiness. The Qur'an declares that only by the remembrance of Allah does the heart become content and thus truly happy. Our real or perceived worldly needs indeed instigate and drive us toward that divine end. For example our need for health drives us to call upon 'The Healer' (*al-Shāfī*). Our need for guidance causes us to seek direction from 'The Guide' (*al-Hādī*). We are in constant need of calling upon Allah in every aspect of our lives, but not always clearly and intentionally. The sincere seeker is constantly focused on a divine name or attribute, which is needed to bring about equilibrium and harmony in life.

The enlightened believer aspires to a point of knowledge where he sees Allah's Attributes in everything and in every situation, realizing that he is truly witnessing his Creator as evident in everything that exists by His grace.

Allah's name and Attributes are the invisible fabric that holds His creations together. His qualities are desired by all created entities. It is His perfection which is sought and adored by all creation. This love is the source of all worship.

1.

اللَّهُ لَا إِلَهَ إِلَّا هُوَ الْحَيُّ الْقَيُّومُ لَا تَأْخُذُهُ سِنَةٌ وَلَا نَوْمٌ لَهُ مَا فِي السَّمَاوَاتِ وَمَا فِي الْأَرْضِ مَن ذَا الَّذِي يَشْفَعُ عِندَهُ إِلَّا بِإِذْنِهِ يَعْلَمُ مَا بَيْنَ أَيْدِيهِمْ وَمَا خَلْفَهُمْ وَلَا يُحِيطُونَ بِشَيْءٍ مِّنْ عِلْمِهِ إِلَّا بِمَا شَاءَ وَسِعَ كُرْسِيُّهُ السَّمَاوَاتِ وَالْأَرْضَ وَلَا يَئُودُهُ حِفْظُهُمَا وَهُوَ الْعَلِيُّ الْعَظِيمُ

Allah, there is no god but Him, the Living, the Self-Sustaining. Neither slumber nor sleep can overtake Him. To Him belongs whatever is in the heavens and the earth. Who can intercede with Him except by His permission? He knows what is before them and what is behind them, while they have no access to knowledge except what He wills. His footstool encompasses the heavens and the earth, and He is never weary of preserving them. He is the Most High, the Immense.

2/255

2.

هُوَ الْأَوَّلُ وَالْآخِرُ وَالظَّاهِرُ وَالْبَاطِنُ وَهُوَ بِكُلِّ شَيْءٍ عَلِيمٌ هُوَ الَّذِي خَلَقَ السَّمَاوَاتِ وَالْأَرْضَ فِي سِتَّةِ أَيَّامٍ ثُمَّ اسْتَوَىٰ عَلَى الْعَرْشِ يَعْلَمُ مَا يَلِجُ فِي الْأَرْضِ وَمَا يَخْرُجُ مِنْهَا وَمَا يَنزِلُ مِنَ السَّمَاءِ وَمَا يَعْرُجُ فِيهَا وَهُوَ مَعَكُمْ أَيْنَ مَا كُنتُمْ وَاللَّهُ بِمَا تَعْمَلُونَ بَصِيرٌ

His glorious Names and Attributes are numerous. They range from the subtlety of life and light to actions such as creation and provision. Mankind can experience many of these Attributes, such as generosity and patience. He is the Absolute Source of all that is praiseworthy.

He is the First, the Last, the Outward and the Inward; and He is the Knower of all things. It is He Who created the heavens and the earth in six days; then He established Himself upon the Throne. He knows all that enters the earth and all that emerges from it, and all that descends from the sky and all that ascends up into it. He is with you wherever you may be, and Allah sees all that you do.

57/3-4

3.

وَلِلَّهِ الْأَسْمَاءُ الْحُسْنَىٰ فَادْعُوهُ بِهَا ۖ وَذَرُوا الَّذِينَ يُلْحِدُونَ فِي أَسْمَائِهِ ۚ سَيُجْزَوْنَ مَا كَانُوا يَعْمَلُونَ

Allah's are the most beautiful names, so invoke Him by them. Leave those who desecrate His names. They will be repaid for what they do.

7/180

Worship of Allah is based on knowledge and love of His qualities, which we are in need of all the time.

4.

قُلِ ادْعُوا اللَّهَ أَوِ ادْعُوا الرَّحْمَٰنَ ۖ أَيًّا مَا تَدْعُوا فَلَهُ الْأَسْمَاءُ الْحُسْنَىٰ ۚ وَلَا تَجْهَرْ بِصَلَاتِكَ وَلَا تُخَافِتْ بِهَا وَابْتَغِ بَيْنَ ذَٰلِكَ سَبِيلًا

Say: Call on Allah or call on the All-Merciful, whichever you call upon, His are the Most Beautiful Names Be not loud of voice in your prayer *(salah)*, nor too quiet, but follow a way between the two.

17/110

5.

اللَّهُ نُورُ السَّمَاوَاتِ وَالْأَرْضِ ۚ مَثَلُ نُورِهِ كَمِشْكَاةٍ فِيهَا مِصْبَاحٌ ۖ الْمِصْبَاحُ فِي زُجَاجَةٍ ۖ الزُّجَاجَةُ كَأَنَّهَا كَوْكَبٌ دُرِّيٌّ يُوقَدُ مِنْ شَجَرَةٍ مُبَارَكَةٍ زَيْتُونَةٍ لَا شَرْقِيَّةٍ وَلَا غَرْبِيَّةٍ يَكَادُ زَيْتُهَا يُضِيءُ وَلَوْ لَمْ تَمْسَسْهُ نَارٌ ۚ نُورٌ عَلَىٰ نُورٍ ۗ يَهْدِي اللَّهُ لِنُورِهِ مَنْ يَشَاءُ ۚ وَيَضْرِبُ اللَّهُ الْأَمْثَالَ لِلنَّاسِ ۗ وَاللَّهُ بِكُلِّ شَيْءٍ عَلِيمٌ

Allah is the Light of the heavens and the earth. The metaphor of His Light is as a niche in which there is a lamp. The lamp is in a glass. The glass is as though it were a brilliant star kindled from a blessed tree, an olive tree, neither of the east nor of the west. Its oil almost glows though no fire has touched it. Light upon Light. Allah guides to His Light whomever He wills, and Allah strikes metaphors for mankind. Allah is the Knower of all things.

24/35

Allah is the original and permanent Light of Lights. Creation comes about as a result of movement and heat, which originate from His Will. His light remains unaltered and is the power behind all creations.

Every creational act is motivated by desire for contentment and tranquility. The ultimate garden of bliss, with its permanent joy, is what all creations desire. Seeking constant happiness originates from this primal motive, the longing for Eden.

6.

اللَّهُ الَّذِي خَلَقَكُمْ ثُمَّ رَزَقَكُمْ ثُمَّ يُمِيتُكُمْ ثُمَّ يُحْيِيكُمْ هَلْ مِن شُرَكَائِكُم مَّن يَفْعَلُ مِن ذَٰلِكُم مِّن شَيْءٍ سُبْحَانَهُ وَتَعَالَىٰ عَمَّا يُشْرِكُونَ

Allah is He Who created you, then provides for you, then causes you to die and then brings you back to life. Are there any of your false gods that do anything like that? Glory be to Him, and may He be exalted above what they associate with Him *(shirk)*.

30/40

7.

يَمْحُو اللَّهُ مَا يَشَاءُ وَيُثْبِتُ وَعِندَهُ أُمُّ الْكِتَابِ

Allah eliminates what He wills and establishes what He wills. With Him is the source of the Book.

13/39

8.

سَبَّحَ لِلَّهِ مَا فِي السَّمَاوَاتِ وَالْأَرْضِ وَهُوَ الْعَزِيزُ الْحَكِيمُ
لَهُ مُلْكُ السَّمَاوَاتِ وَالْأَرْضِ يُحْيِي وَيُمِيتُ وَهُوَ عَلَىٰ كُلِّ شَيْءٍ قَدِيرٌ

Whatever is in the heavens and the earth glorifies Allah, and He is the Almighty, the All-Wise. His is the Kingdom of the heavens and the earth; He gives life and causes death. He is All - powerful and able to do all things.

57/1-2

No creation can ever fully realize the magnificence of the Creator or the extent of His glory, constant mercy and love. He is the All-Knowing and All-Forgiving, ever present and ever generous.

Allah

9.

وَلِلَّهِ مَا فِي السَّمَاوَاتِ وَمَا فِي الْأَرْضِ وَإِلَى اللَّهِ تُرْجَعُ الْأُمُورُ

To Allah belongs whatever is in the heavens and whatever is in the earth; and to Allah all matters return.

3/109

10.

مَا قَدَرُوا اللَّهَ حَقَّ قَدْرِهِ إِنَّ اللَّهَ لَقَوِيٌّ عَزِيزٌ

They do not measure Allah with His rightful measure. Truly Allah is Eminently-Strong, Almighty.

22/74

11.

إِنَّ رَبَّكَ وَاسِعُ الْمَغْفِرَةِ هُوَ أَعْلَمُ بِكُمْ إِذْ أَنْشَأَكُمْ مِنَ الْأَرْضِ وَإِذْ أَنْتُمْ أَجِنَّةٌ فِي بُطُونِ أُمَّهَاتِكُمْ فَلَا تُزَكُّوا أَنْفُسَكُمْ هُوَ أَعْلَمُ بِمَنِ اتَّقَى

...Certainly your Lord is vast in forgiveness. He is most aware of you; He has created you from the earth, and you were embryos hidden in the wombs of your mothers. Therefore, do not claim purity for yourselves. He is best aware of whoever is in cautious awareness *(taqwā)*.

53/32

12.

غَافِرِ الذَّنْبِ وَقَابِلِ التَّوْبِ شَدِيدِ الْعِقَابِ ذِي الطَّوْلِ لَا إِلَهَ إِلَّا هُوَ إِلَيْهِ الْمَصِيرُ

The Forgiver of Sin, the Acceptor of Repentance, the Severe in Retribution, the Bountiful; there is no God but Him. To Him is the final destination.

40/3

This world is a brief abode and opportunity for the self to awaken to its origin of light beyond physical and material limitation. The end of life on this earth is the return of the soul and spirit to a zone of consciousness without veils or illusions.

The path to this awakening is based on denial of the ego and lower self by constant awareness and reflection.

This earthly life is only a prelude for the return to our original heavenly abode.

Only when we see all existence emanating from Him, sustained by Him, and returning to Him will we realize His unique Oneness, Omnipotence and Omnipresence. Thus will we become truly content at heart with the perfect Lord.

13.

اللَّهُ الَّذِي جَعَلَ لَكُمُ الْأَرْضَ قَرَارًا وَالسَّمَاءَ بِنَاءً وَصَوَّرَكُمْ فَأَحْسَنَ صُوَرَكُمْ وَرَزَقَكُم مِّنَ الطَّيِّبَاتِ ذَٰلِكُمُ اللَّهُ رَبُّكُمْ فَتَبَارَكَ اللَّهُ رَبُّ الْعَالَمِينَ

It is Allah who made the earth for you as a dwelling place and the sky as a canopy; He fashioned you and perfected your shapes, and He has provided you with good things. Such is Allah, your Lord. So blessed is Allah, the Lord of the Worlds.

40/64

14.

قُلْ هُوَ اللَّهُ أَحَدٌ
اللَّهُ الصَّمَدُ
لَمْ يَلِدْ وَلَمْ يُولَدْ
وَلَمْ يَكُن لَّهُ كُفُوًا أَحَدٌ

Say: He is Allah, the One. Allah the Eternal. He does not beget, nor is He begotten; and there is none comparable to Him.

112/1-4

15.

وَمَا قَدَرُوا اللَّهَ حَقَّ قَدْرِهِ وَالْأَرْضُ جَمِيعًا قَبْضَتُهُ يَوْمَ الْقِيَامَةِ وَالسَّمَاوَاتُ مَطْوِيَّاتٌ بِيَمِينِهِ سُبْحَانَهُ وَتَعَالَىٰ عَمَّا يُشْرِكُونَ

They have not estimated and esteemed Allah with His true measure. The entire earth shall be in His grip on the Day of Resurrection, and the heavens will be rolled up in His right hand. Glory be to Him, and exalted is He above all that they associate with Him.

39/67

CHAPTER THREE

ALLAH'S WAYS

The verses in this chapter describe the patterns of existence and their meanings and destinies. All beings, in reality, seek the eternal Divine Perfection, either knowingly or not.

Allah's ways (*sunnah*) include His laws, His decrees and whatever governs the seen and unseen. Allah created all existences in pairs and opposites. Every entity in existence is balanced and rooted in its opposite. His decrees do not change, but individual societal destinies change according to the paths they take.

Allah has designed the basic human primal pattern so that it seeks Eternal Light and a state of paradise. All creation desires and adores Allah's Attributes as He is the Source and Sustainer of all existence, and all things return to him. Allah guides to Himself, for the truth is that there is none other than Him. There is no god but Allah, and Muhammad is His messenger.

The entire cosmos is based on divine unity (*tawhīd*). He has designed all creations in a manner that the realization of each one's potential and completion is through submission and celebration of His eternal presence. In every circumstance He knows the appropriate way to reorientate anything towards Himself. His decrees are all-merciful and lead to Him by Him. The desired destiny is attained when we follow the original and ultimate purpose of existence, which is to know and worship Him.

The Creator is one, the First before anything and the Last after everything. He is the most evident and yet veiled behind His Attributes. He has created all existential realities within time/space in pairs or opposites such as life and death, good and bad, night and day.

The way of Messengers, Prophets and the divine Books are the maps and pathways that are natural and enduring. Thus, they are to be followed by those seeking the truth, which is forever constant.

1.

تَبَارَكَ الَّذِي بِيَدِهِ الْمُلْكُ وَهُوَ عَلَىٰ كُلِّ شَيْءٍ قَدِيرٌ الَّذِي خَلَقَ الْمَوْتَ وَالْحَيَاةَ لِيَبْلُوَكُمْ أَيُّكُمْ أَحْسَنُ عَمَلًا وَهُوَ الْعَزِيزُ الْغَفُورُ الَّذِي خَلَقَ سَبْعَ سَمَاوَاتٍ طِبَاقًا مَّا تَرَىٰ فِي خَلْقِ الرَّحْمَٰنِ مِن تَفَاوُتٍ فَارْجِعِ الْبَصَرَ هَلْ تَرَىٰ مِن فُطُورٍ ثُمَّ ارْجِعِ الْبَصَرَ كَرَّتَيْنِ يَنقَلِبْ إِلَيْكَ الْبَصَرُ خَاسِئًا وَهُوَ حَسِيرٌ

Blessed is He who has the Kingdom in His hands, and He is able to do all things. He who has created death and life that He may try you, which of you is best in action. And He is the Almighty, All-Forgiving. Who has created seven heavens in layers? You cannot see any faults in the creation of the All-Merciful. Then look again, can you see any rifts? Look again repeatedly, your sight will return to you weakened and humbled.

67/1-4

2.

وَلَوْ شَاءَ اللَّهُ لَجَعَلَكُمْ أُمَّةً وَاحِدَةً وَلَٰكِن لِّيَبْلُوَكُمْ فِي مَا آتَاكُمْ فَاسْتَبِقُوا الْخَيْرَاتِ إِلَى اللَّهِ مَرْجِعُكُمْ جَمِيعًا فَيُنَبِّئُكُم بِمَا كُنتُمْ فِيهِ تَخْتَلِفُونَ

...Had Allah willed He would have made you one community, but He wanted to try you by that which He has given you; so compete in good works. To Allah you will all return, and He will inform you about that which you differed.

5/48

3.

وَلِكُلِّ أُمَّةٍ جَعَلْنَا مَنسَكًا لِّيَذْكُرُوا اسْمَ اللَّهِ عَلَىٰ مَا رَزَقَهُم مِّن بَهِيمَةِ الْأَنْعَامِ فَإِلَٰهُكُمْ إِلَٰهٌ وَاحِدٌ فَلَهُ أَسْلِمُوا وَبَشِّرِ الْمُخْبِتِينَ الَّذِينَ إِذَا ذُكِرَ اللَّهُ وَجِلَتْ قُلُوبُهُمْ وَالصَّابِرِينَ عَلَىٰ مَا أَصَابَهُمْ وَالْمُقِيمِي الصَّلَاةِ وَمِمَّا رَزَقْنَاهُمْ يُنفِقُونَ

And for every nation We had appointed a ritual so that they may invoke the name of Allah over the provision of livestock that He had given them. And your God is one God, therefore surrender to Him, and give good news to the humble hearted. Whose hearts submit when Allah is mentioned, and who are steadfast in whatever afflicts them, establishing prayer *(salāt)* and spending of what We have bestowed upon them.

22/34-35

The purpose of all creation is to know the Creator and follow His light by surrendering to it and living joyfully by it.

4.

وَلَوِ اتَّبَعَ الْحَقُّ أَهْوَاءَهُمْ لَفَسَدَتِ السَّمَاوَاتُ وَالْأَرْضُ وَمَن فِيهِنَّ بَلْ أَتَيْنَاهُم بِذِكْرِهِمْ فَهُمْ عَن ذِكْرِهِم مُّعْرِضُونَ

And if the truth had followed their whims, then the heavens and earth and whoever is in them would be corrupted. Indeed, We have given them their Reminder, but from their Reminder they turn away.

23/71

Through the light of a pure heart, the Merciful will lead creation towards its fulfilled destiny.

He is the All Powerful, the Majestic, bestowing natural bounds and limitations for all of His creations.

5.

إِن يَشَأْ يُذْهِبْكُمْ أَيُّهَا ٱلنَّاسُ وَيَأْتِ بِـَٔاخَرِينَ وَكَانَ ٱللَّهُ عَلَىٰ ذَٰلِكَ قَدِيرًا

If He wills, He can remove you, O people, and bring forth others. Allah is most able to do that.

4/133

6.

إِنَّ بَطْشَ رَبِّكَ لَشَدِيدٌ ۝ إِنَّهُۥ هُوَ يُبْدِئُ وَيُعِيدُ ۝ وَهُوَ ٱلْغَفُورُ ٱلْوَدُودُ ۝ ذُو ٱلْعَرْشِ ٱلْمَجِيدُ ۝ فَعَّالٌ لِّمَا يُرِيدُ ۝

Enlightened human beings with true insight witness the boundless within the limited, acknowledging the ever-present Lord of the Universe.

Truly, the punishment of your Lord is stern. It is He who originates and regenerates, And He is the All - Forgiving, the All - Loving, Possessor of the Glorious Throne, Doer of what He wills.

85/12-16

7.

تِلْكَ حُدُودُ ٱللَّهِ فَلَا تَقْرَبُوهَا كَذَٰلِكَ يُبَيِّنُ ٱللَّهُ ءَايَٰتِهِۦ لِلنَّاسِ لَعَلَّهُمْ يَتَّقُونَ

...These are the limits imposed by Allah so do not approach them. Thus Allah makes his signs clear to mankind so that they may be in cautious awareness.

2/187

8.

الم
أَحَسِبَ ٱلنَّاسُ أَن يُتْرَكُوٓا۟ أَن يَقُولُوٓا۟ ءَامَنَّا وَهُمْ لَا يُفْتَنُونَ

The purpose of human creation is to be at the altar of the One All-Encompassing, ever present Master, read His signs and follow His decrees.

Alif Lām Mīm. Do people imagine that they will be left to say 'We believe,' and they will not be tested with affliction?

29/1-2

9.

فَإِذَا مَسَّ الْإِنسَانَ ضُرٌّ دَعَانَا ثُمَّ إِذَا خَوَّلْنَاهُ نِعْمَةً مِّنَّا قَالَ إِنَّمَا أُوتِيتُهُ عَلَىٰ عِلْمٍ ۚ بَلْ هِيَ فِتْنَةٌ وَلَٰكِنَّ أَكْثَرَهُمْ لَا يَعْلَمُونَ

When harm touches man he calls on Us; then when We have granted him a benefit from Us, he says: This has come to me through my knowledge. In fact it is a trial, but most of them do not understand.

39/49

He provides what is needed for the journey to Him, pardoning, forgiving, and ever-patient. He is all encompassing and to him all dominions return.

10.

اللَّهُ يَبْسُطُ الرِّزْقَ لِمَن يَشَاءُ مِنْ عِبَادِهِ وَيَقْدِرُ لَهُ ۚ إِنَّ اللَّهَ بِكُلِّ شَيْءٍ عَلِيمٌ

Allah expands provision for whom He wills among His bondsmen, and He restricts it (for whom he wills). Certainly, Allah has knowledge of all things.

29/62

His laws and decrees prevail over His universe according to His perfect commands and perfect justice.

11.

يُعَذِّبُ مَن يَشَاءُ وَيَرْحَمُ مَن يَشَاءُ ۖ وَإِلَيْهِ تُقْلَبُونَ

He punishes whom He wills and shows mercy to whom He wills, and to Him you will be returned.

29/21

12.

وَرَبُّكَ الْغَفُورُ ذُو الرَّحْمَةِ ۖ لَوْ يُؤَاخِذُهُم بِمَا كَسَبُوا لَعَجَّلَ لَهُمُ الْعَذَابَ ۚ بَل لَّهُم مَّوْعِدٌ لَّن يَجِدُوا مِن دُونِهِ مَوْئِلًا

Your Lord is the Forgiving and the Possessor of Mercy. If He had taken them to task for what they had earned, He would have hastened their punishment. But there is an appointed term from which they will find no escape.

18/58

Thus no intention or action goes unheeded. As human beings we are responsible for what we do at all times.

All heavenly and earthly bodies move and rotate in adoration of His Majesty. Creation aspires to His perfection, beauty and ever-presence.

The humbled self with a pure heart that strives towards Him with certainty of His mercy will be guided to witnessing His presence at all times and in all places.

Those who are most submissive to Him are the most noble in His eyes.

13.

وَمَا مِنْ غَائِبَةٍ فِي السَّمَاءِ وَالْأَرْضِ إِلَّا فِي كِتَابٍ مُبِينٍ

And there is nothing hidden in the heavens or the earth but that it is in a clear Book.

27/75

14.

يَا بُنَيَّ إِنَّهَا إِنْ تَكُ مِثْقَالَ حَبَّةٍ مِنْ خَرْدَلٍ فَتَكُنْ فِي صَخْرَةٍ أَوْ فِي السَّمَاوَاتِ أَوْ فِي الْأَرْضِ يَأْتِ بِهَا اللَّهُ إِنَّ اللَّهَ لَطِيفٌ خَبِيرٌ

O my son (Luqman's son), even if something weighs as little as the grain of a mustard seed and is inside a rock, or anywhere in the heavens or the earth, Allah will bring it forth. Truly, Allah is the Subtle, All-Aware.

31/16

15.

أَلَمْ تَرَ أَنَّ اللَّهَ يَسْجُدُ لَهُ مَنْ فِي السَّمَاوَاتِ وَمَنْ فِي الْأَرْضِ وَالشَّمْسُ وَالْقَمَرُ وَالنُّجُومُ وَالْجِبَالُ وَالشَّجَرُ وَالدَّوَابُّ وَكَثِيرٌ مِنَ النَّاسِ وَكَثِيرٌ حَقَّ عَلَيْهِ الْعَذَابُ وَمَنْ يُهِنِ اللَّهُ فَمَا لَهُ مِنْ مُكْرِمٍ إِنَّ اللَّهَ يَفْعَلُ مَا يَشَاءُ

Do you not see that whatever is in the heavens and the earth, and the sun, and the moon, and the stars, the mountains, the trees, the beasts, and many of mankind all bow in worship to Allah. Most of them are deserving of punishment. He whom Allah scorns will have no one to honour him. Certainly, Allah does what He will.

22/18

16.

وَنُرِيدُ أَن نَّمُنَّ عَلَى الَّذِينَ اسْتُضْعِفُوا فِي الْأَرْضِ وَنَجْعَلَهُمْ أَئِمَّةً وَنَجْعَلَهُمُ الْوَارِثِينَ

We desire to show favour to those who are oppressed in the earth, to make them leaders and to make them the inheritors.

28/5

17.

إِنَّ اللَّهَ لَا يُغَيِّرُ مَا بِقَوْمٍ حَتَّىٰ يُغَيِّرُوا مَا بِأَنفُسِهِمْ وَإِذَا أَرَادَ اللَّهُ بِقَوْمٍ سُوءًا فَلَا مَرَدَّ لَهُ وَمَا لَهُم مِّن دُونِهِ مِن وَالٍ

...Truly, Allah does not change the condition of people until they change what is in themselves. If Allah intends misfortune for a people, there is no averting it, nor will they have a protector apart from Him.

13/11

18.

وَالَّذِينَ جَاهَدُوا فِينَا لَنَهْدِيَنَّهُمْ سُبُلَنَا وَإِنَّ اللَّهَ لَمَعَ الْمُحْسِنِينَ

As for those who strive for Us, We will guide them to Our path. Truly, Allah is with those who do good.

29/69

19.

وَمَا خَلَقْتُ الْجِنَّ وَالْإِنسَ إِلَّا لِيَعْبُدُونِ

I have not created the invisible entities (*jinn*) and mankind except that they may worship Me.

51/56

He is the original Light of all that is in the heavens and the earth. Human light or spirit has its source in the original Divine Light. Thus we all belong to Him and in all states are sustained by Him.

The human spirit is heavenly, caught in a terrestrial form seeking harmony, contentment and eternal joy. In this world we only experience glimpses of the desired states of perfection.

20.

$$\text{وَمَن لَّمْ يَجْعَلِ اللَّهُ لَهُ نُورًا فَمَا لَهُ مِن نُّورٍ}$$

...Whoever Allah has not given light to, for him there is no light.

24/40

21.

$$\text{وَمَن كَانَ فِي هَٰذِهِ أَعْمَىٰ فَهُوَ فِي الْآخِرَةِ أَعْمَىٰ وَأَضَلُّ سَبِيلًا}$$

Whoever is blind here will be blind in the hereafter, and yet further astray from the path.

17/72

22.

$$\text{وَفِي الْأَرْضِ آيَاتٌ لِّلْمُوقِنِينَ}$$
$$\text{وَفِي أَنفُسِكُمْ أَفَلَا تُبْصِرُونَ}$$
$$\text{وَفِي السَّمَاءِ رِزْقُكُمْ وَمَا تُوعَدُونَ}$$

And in the earth there are signs for the people of certainty, and in yourselves. Do you not see? And in the heaven is your provision and what you are promised.

51/20

This world is a small sample and prelude for the unseen worlds. Wherever we look and contemplate we witness signs and traces of divine power and presence.

Allah's Ways

23.

وَمِنْ ءَايَـٰتِهِۦٓ أَنْ خَلَقَ لَكُم مِّنْ أَنفُسِكُمْ أَزْوَٰجًا لِّتَسْكُنُوٓا۟ إِلَيْهَا وَجَعَلَ بَيْنَكُم مَّوَدَّةً وَرَحْمَةً ۚ إِنَّ فِى ذَٰلِكَ لَـَٔايَـٰتٍ لِّقَوْمٍ يَتَفَكَّرُونَ وَمِنْ ءَايَـٰتِهِۦ خَلْقُ ٱلسَّمَـٰوَٰتِ وَٱلْأَرْضِ وَٱخْتِلَـٰفُ أَلْسِنَتِكُمْ وَأَلْوَٰنِكُمْ ۚ إِنَّ فِى ذَٰلِكَ لَـَٔايَـٰتٍ لِّلْعَـٰلِمِينَ وَمِنْ ءَايَـٰتِهِۦ مَنَامُكُم بِٱلَّيْلِ وَٱلنَّهَارِ وَٱبْتِغَآؤُكُم مِّن فَضْلِهِۦٓ ۚ إِنَّ فِى ذَٰلِكَ لَـَٔايَـٰتٍ لِّقَوْمٍ يَسْمَعُونَ وَمِنْ ءَايَـٰتِهِۦ يُرِيكُمُ ٱلْبَرْقَ خَوْفًا وَطَمَعًا وَيُنَزِّلُ مِنَ ٱلسَّمَآءِ مَآءً فَيُحْىِۦ بِهِ ٱلْأَرْضَ بَعْدَ مَوْتِهَآ ۚ إِنَّ فِى ذَٰلِكَ لَـَٔايَـٰتٍ لِّقَوْمٍ يَعْقِلُونَ

Among His signs is that: He created for you mates from among yourselves that you might find tranquility in them, and He ordained between you love and mercy. Indeed, in this are signs for people who reflect. Among His signs is the creation of the heavens and the earth, and the difference of your tongues and colors. Indeed, in this are signs for those possessed of knowledge. Among His signs is your slumber at night and in the daytime and your seeking His bounty. Indeed, in this are signs for people who truly hear. Among His signs is that He shows you the lightning for fear and for hope; and He sends down water from the sky, thereby bringing life to the earth after its death. Indeed, in this are signs for people who understand

30/21-24

24.

وَهُوَ ٱلَّذِى يَبْدَؤُا۟ ٱلْخَلْقَ ثُمَّ يُعِيدُهُۥ وَهُوَ أَهْوَنُ عَلَيْهِ ۚ وَلَهُ ٱلْمَثَلُ ٱلْأَعْلَىٰ فِى ٱلسَّمَـٰوَٰتِ وَٱلْأَرْضِ ۚ وَهُوَ ٱلْعَزِيزُ ٱلْحَكِيمُ

It is He who originates the creation, then reproduces it, and it is easy for Him. His is the Exalted State in the heavens and earth. He is the Almighty, the All Wise.

30/27

Everything in existence occurs in pairs and opposites and seeks stability. The physical world is caught in His web of cause and effect energized by His unique Oneness.

He is the Most Generous and Just, but most human beings are veiled by their personal and cultural habits and misconceptions. Thus we deprive ourselves from the joy of witnessing His Glorious Presence.

Every creation is allotted its appropriate provision and time on earth according to His laws and decrees. All that is needed is to read and follow His signs.

Nothing ever occurs in existence unless it is according to His laws and prescribed ways. He is constant, the Ever-Present and the All-Knowing.

Constriction and limitation are aspects of His Mercy and Power to humble creation and to increase their awareness of His purpose and Might.

Although everyone will experience death and departure from this world, most people try to forget or ignore this certainty. For the believer, remembrance of the Hereafter lightens the burdens of this world and brings about greater faith, patience and spiritual growth and sensitivity.

25.

إِنَّ اللَّهَ لَا يَظْلِمُ النَّاسَ شَيْئًا وَلَٰكِنَّ النَّاسَ أَنفُسَهُمْ يَظْلِمُونَ

Truly, Allah does not wrong mankind in any way, but mankind wrong themselves.

10/44

26.

وَمَا مِن دَابَّةٍ فِي الْأَرْضِ إِلَّا عَلَى اللَّهِ رِزْقُهَا وَيَعْلَمُ مُسْتَقَرَّهَا وَمُسْتَوْدَعَهَا كُلٌّ فِي كِتَابٍ مُّبِينٍ

There is no creature in the earth but that its sustenance depends upon Allah. He knows where it lives and where it dies. All is in a clear Book.

11/6

27.

اللَّهُ الَّذِي جَعَلَ لَكُمُ اللَّيْلَ لِتَسْكُنُوا فِيهِ وَالنَّهَارَ مُبْصِرًا إِنَّ اللَّهَ لَذُو فَضْلٍ عَلَى النَّاسِ وَلَٰكِنَّ أَكْثَرَ النَّاسِ لَا يَشْكُرُونَ

Allah made the night for you to rest and the day for seeing. Truly, Allah is full of grace to mankind, yet most of mankind does not give thanks.

40/61

28.

لِّئَلَّا يَعْلَمَ أَهْلُ الْكِتَابِ أَلَّا يَقْدِرُونَ عَلَىٰ شَيْءٍ مِّن فَضْلِ اللَّهِ وَأَنَّ الْفَضْلَ بِيَدِ اللَّهِ يُؤْتِيهِ مَن يَشَاءُ وَاللَّهُ ذُو الْفَضْلِ الْعَظِيمِ

So that the People of the Book may know that they have no power whatsoever over the Grace of Allah, and that His Grace is entirely in His hand to bestow upon whomsoever He wills. And Allah is the possessor of Great Bounty.

57/29

29.

مَا أَصَابَ مِن مُّصِيبَةٍ فِي الْأَرْضِ وَلَا فِي أَنفُسِكُمْ إِلَّا فِي كِتَابٍ مِّن قَبْلِ أَن نَّبْرَأَهَا إِنَّ ذَٰلِكَ عَلَى اللَّهِ يَسِيرٌ

Nothing occurs, either in the earth or in yourselves, without its being in a Book before We bring it into existence. That is easy for Allah.

57/22

The All-Merciful brings about constriction and difficulty so that we are humbled and call upon Him for guidance and forgiveness. Afflictions are part of His mercy, which is recognized by those who trust and reflect with insight.

30.

وَلَوْ رَحِمْنَاهُمْ وَكَشَفْنَا مَا بِهِم مِّن ضُرٍّ لَّلَجُّوا فِي طُغْيَانِهِمْ يَعْمَهُونَ

And if We bestowed mercy on them and relieved them of the harm afflicting them, they would persist in their obstinacy, wandering blindly on.

23/75

31.

وَإِذَا أَذَقْنَا النَّاسَ رَحْمَةً مِّن بَعْدِ ضَرَّاءَ مَسَّتْهُمْ إِذَا لَهُم مَّكْرٌ فِي آيَاتِنَا قُلِ اللَّهُ أَسْرَعُ مَكْرًا إِنَّ رُسُلَنَا يَكْتُبُونَ مَا تَمْكُرُونَ

And when We cause people to taste mercy after some adversity which afflicted them, they plot against Our signs. Say: Allah is quicker in plotting. Surely, Our messengers write down what you plot.

10/21

Those who love the material world and its fleeting pleasures will receive their share of its ease, but they reach the hereafter bereft and unprepared.

32.

وَلَنَبْلُوَنَّكُم بِشَيْءٍ مِّنَ الْخَوْفِ وَالْجُوعِ وَنَقْصٍ مِّنَ الْأَمْوَالِ وَالْأَنفُسِ وَالثَّمَرَاتِ وَبَشِّرِ الصَّابِرِينَ

We shall try you with fear and hunger, with loss of wealth, lives and crops; but give glad tidings to those who are steadfast.

2/155

The sincere seeker desires safe passage in this world and access to His light at all times.

Allah's wish is for creation to be guided and to follow the prescribed path towards the vast landscape of His celestial horizons of the hereafter.

Arrogance and the illusion of independence in this world will only increase the darkness and veils for those who are misguided.

Allah's commands and channels of power are endless. His light illumines all existence, seen and unseen. Indeed, it is by Allah's light and knowledge that we discern darkness and ignorance in this transitory world and its deceptions.

33.

كُلُّ نَفْسٍ ذَآئِقَةُ ٱلْمَوْتِ وَإِنَّمَا تُوَفَّوْنَ أُجُورَكُمْ يَوْمَ ٱلْقِيَٰمَةِ فَمَن زُحْزِحَ عَنِ ٱلنَّارِ وَأُدْخِلَ ٱلْجَنَّةَ فَقَدْ فَازَ وَمَا ٱلْحَيَوٰةُ ٱلدُّنْيَآ إِلَّا مَتَٰعُ ٱلْغُرُورِ

Every soul will taste death, and you will be given your reward on the Day of Resurrection. Then whoever is removed from the Fire and admitted to the Garden, has indeed triumphed. The life of this world is an illusory pleasure.

3/185

34.

وَلَنَبْلُوَنَّكُمْ حَتَّىٰ نَعْلَمَ ٱلْمُجَٰهِدِينَ مِنكُمْ وَٱلصَّٰبِرِينَ وَنَبْلُوَا۟ أَخْبَارَكُمْ

We shall try you till We know those of you who strive hard and are patient and steadfast. We will test your record of deeds

47/31

35.

مَن كَانَ يُرِيدُ ٱلْحَيَوٰةَ ٱلدُّنْيَا وَزِينَتَهَا نُوَفِّ إِلَيْهِمْ أَعْمَٰلَهُمْ فِيهَا وَهُمْ فِيهَا لَا يُبْخَسُونَ أُو۟لَٰٓئِكَ ٱلَّذِينَ لَيْسَ لَهُمْ فِى ٱلْءَاخِرَةِ إِلَّا ٱلنَّارُ وَحَبِطَ مَا صَنَعُوا۟ فِيهَا وَبَٰطِلٌ مَّا كَانُوا۟ يَعْمَلُونَ

Whoever desires the life of this world and its finery, We shall repay them by their deeds in it, and they will not be wronged. There is nothing in the Hereafter for them but the Fire. What they have achieved here will come to naught; their deeds are in vain.

11/15-16

36.

وَاكْتُبْ لَنَا فِى هَٰذِهِ الدُّنْيَا حَسَنَةً وَفِى الْآخِرَةِ إِنَّا هُدْنَا إِلَيْكَ قَالَ عَذَابِى أُصِيبُ بِهِ مَنْ أَشَاءُ وَرَحْمَتِى وَسِعَتْ كُلَّ شَىْءٍ فَسَأَكْتُبُهَا لِلَّذِينَ يَتَّقُونَ وَيُؤْتُونَ الزَّكَاةَ وَالَّذِينَ هُم بِآيَاتِنَا يُؤْمِنُونَ

He said, 'As for My punishment, I strike with it whomever I will and my mercy extends to all things. I will prescribe it for those who have cautious awareness *(taqwā)*, purify by alms *(zakāt)*, and believe in Our clear Signs.

7/156

The sincere seekers will constantly ask for and desire His mercy and act selflessly and with constant caution and awareness.

37.

يُرِيدُ اللَّهُ لِيُبَيِّنَ لَكُمْ وَيَهْدِيَكُمْ سُنَنَ الَّذِينَ مِن قَبْلِكُمْ وَيَتُوبَ عَلَيْكُمْ وَاللَّهُ عَلِيمٌ حَكِيمٌ

Allah wants to explain to you and guide you by the example of those who were before you, and would turn to you in mercy. Allah is All-Knowing, All-Wise.

4/26

Those who are cautious, aware and patient will be guided through conflict and confusion towards knowledge and trustful submission.

38.

وَيَسْتَعْجِلُونَكَ بِالْعَذَابِ وَلَوْلَا أَجَلٌ مُّسَمًّى لَّجَاءَهُمُ الْعَذَابُ وَلَيَأْتِيَنَّهُم بَغْتَةً وَهُمْ لَا يَشْعُرُونَ

They ask you to hasten the punishment. If it were not a stipulated term, the punishment would have come to them already. It will come upon them suddenly when they are not expecting it.

29/53

Those in fearful awareness will experience the garden of inner contentment in this world and a boundless paradise in the next.

The Lord is in control of every moment and event and He guides illumined hearts. As for the arrogant ones, they follow their destiny of doom. His decrees and ways are infinite and no account can contain them.

Human beings always have inherent weaknesses and needs, and He is the One who gives and spreads His light.

39.

ٱسْتِكْبَارًا فِي ٱلْأَرْضِ وَمَكْرَ ٱلسَّيِّئِ وَلَا يَحِيقُ ٱلْمَكْرُ ٱلسَّيِّئُ إِلَّا بِأَهْلِهِ فَهَلْ يَنظُرُونَ إِلَّا سُنَّتَ ٱلْأَوَّلِينَ فَلَن تَجِدَ لِسُنَّتِ ٱللَّهِ تَبْدِيلًا وَلَن تَجِدَ لِسُنَّتِ ٱللَّهِ تَحْوِيلًا

The evil plot only envelops those who make it. Then can they expect anything but the treatment of the ancients? You will not find any change in Allah's way, nor will you find any change in Allah's course.

35/43

40.

قُل لَّوْ كَانَ ٱلْبَحْرُ مِدَادًا لِّكَلِمَاتِ رَبِّي لَنَفِدَ ٱلْبَحْرُ قَبْلَ أَن تَنفَدَ كَلِمَاتُ رَبِّي وَلَوْ جِئْنَا بِمِثْلِهِ مَدَدًا

Say: If the sea was ink for the Words of my Lord, the sea would surely be exhausted before the Words of my Lord finished, even though We brought the likes of it to help.

18/109

41.

يُرِيدُونَ أَن يُطْفِئُوا نُورَ ٱللَّهِ بِأَفْوَاهِهِمْ وَيَأْبَى ٱللَّهُ إِلَّا أَن يُتِمَّ نُورَهُ وَلَوْ كَرِهَ ٱلْكَافِرُونَ

They desire to extinguish the Light of Allah with their mouths, but Allah will not allow (anything) except the completion of His Light, even though the disbelievers detest it.

9/32

42.

وَمَن يَتَّقِ ٱللَّهَ يَجْعَل لَّهُ مَخْرَجًا

And whoever has cautious awareness of Allah, He will open a way.

65/2

43.

$$\text{فَإِنَّ مَعَ الْعُسْرِ يُسْرًا}$$
$$\text{إِنَّ مَعَ الْعُسْرِ يُسْرًا}$$

Certainly, with hardship there is ease,
Certainly, with hardship there is ease.

94/5-6

44.

$$\text{وَلِمَنْ خَافَ مَقَامَ رَبِّهِ جَنَّتَانِ}$$
$$\text{فَبِأَيِّ آلَاءِ رَبِّكُمَا تُكَذِّبَانِ}$$

For he who fears the station of his Lord there are two gardens. Then which of the favours of your Lord will you deny?

55/46-47

45.

$$\text{وَالضُّحَىٰ ۝ وَاللَّيْلِ إِذَا سَجَىٰ ۝ مَا وَدَّعَكَ رَبُّكَ وَمَا قَلَىٰ ۝ وَلَلْآخِرَةُ خَيْرٌ لَّكَ مِنَ الْأُولَىٰ ۝ وَلَسَوْفَ يُعْطِيكَ رَبُّكَ فَتَرْضَىٰ ۝ أَلَمْ يَجِدْكَ يَتِيمًا فَآوَىٰ ۝ وَوَجَدَكَ ضَالًّا فَهَدَىٰ ۝ وَوَجَدَكَ عَائِلًا فَأَغْنَىٰ ۝ فَأَمَّا الْيَتِيمَ فَلَا تَقْهَرْ ۝ وَأَمَّا السَّائِلَ فَلَا تَنْهَرْ ۝ وَأَمَّا بِنِعْمَةِ رَبِّكَ فَحَدِّثْ ۝}$$

By the brightness of the morning star, And by the night when it is still, Your Lord has not forsaken you, nor is He displeased. And truly the latter state will be better for you than the former, and truly your Lord will give you so that you will be content. Did He not find you an orphan and protect you? Did He not find you wandering and direct you? Did He not find you destitute and enrich you? Therefore, do not oppress the orphan, and do not drive away the beggar. As for the favours of your Lord, proclaim them.

93/1-11

He is the source and essence and all great attributes and qualities belong to Him. Our duty is to follow His decrees appropriately as the great prophets and enlightened ones did so that we come to recognize the Ever-Present one in all situations.

Every experience or state is one of two opposites. There is no goodness without the seeds of evil in it. There is no generosity without the root of meanness in it. The enlightened being only witnesses Allah's generosity in all occurrences and thus is exposed to the two gardens of meaning and experience.

He does not wish to punish us. It is we who bring about that experiential conclusion by following inappropriate ways. His generosity is such that once we recognize our folly and waywardness, we can correct our ways. He is the Ever-Present, Ever-Forgiving.

46.

ثُمَّ أَنزَلَ عَلَيْكُم مِّنۢ بَعْدِ ٱلْغَمِّ أَمَنَةً نُّعَاسًا يَغْشَىٰ طَآئِفَةً مِّنكُمْ ۖ وَطَآئِفَةٌ قَدْ أَهَمَّتْهُمْ أَنفُسُهُمْ يَظُنُّونَ بِٱللَّهِ غَيْرَ ٱلْحَقِّ ظَنَّ ٱلْجَٰهِلِيَّةِ ۖ يَقُولُونَ هَل لَّنَا مِنَ ٱلْأَمْرِ مِن شَىْءٍ ۗ قُلْ إِنَّ ٱلْأَمْرَ كُلَّهُۥ لِلَّهِ ۗ يُخْفُونَ فِىٓ أَنفُسِهِم مَّا لَا يُبْدُونَ لَكَ ۖ يَقُولُونَ لَوْ كَانَ لَنَا مِنَ ٱلْأَمْرِ شَىْءٌ مَّا قُتِلْنَا هَٰهُنَا ۗ قُل لَّوْ كُنتُمْ فِى بُيُوتِكُمْ لَبَرَزَ ٱلَّذِينَ كُتِبَ عَلَيْهِمُ ٱلْقَتْلُ إِلَىٰ مَضَاجِعِهِمْ ۖ وَلِيَبْتَلِىَ ٱللَّهُ مَا فِى صُدُورِكُمْ وَلِيُمَحِّصَ مَا فِى قُلُوبِكُمْ ۗ وَٱللَّهُ عَلِيمٌۢ بِذَاتِ ٱلصُّدُورِ

Then after the grief, He sent down safety for you, slumber overcoming a party of you, while another party, who were concerned about themselves, thought other than the truth about Allah, thoughts belonging to the Time of Ignorance. They said: Have we any part in the affair? Say: The affair belongs entirely to Allah. They conceal within themselves that which they do not reveal to you, saying: Had we had any part in the affair we would not have been slain here. Say: Even if you had been inside your houses, those of you who decreed to be killed would have rushed to where they would lie (dead). So that Allah might test what is in your breast and purge what is in your hearts. Allah is Knower of what is hidden in the breasts (of men).

3/154

47.

وَعَدَ اللَّهُ الَّذِينَ آمَنُوا مِنكُمْ وَعَمِلُوا الصَّالِحَاتِ لَيَسْتَخْلِفَنَّهُمْ فِي الْأَرْضِ كَمَا اسْتَخْلَفَ الَّذِينَ مِن قَبْلِهِمْ وَلَيُمَكِّنَنَّ لَهُمْ دِينَهُمُ الَّذِي ارْتَضَىٰ لَهُمْ وَلَيُبَدِّلَنَّهُم مِّن بَعْدِ خَوْفِهِمْ أَمْنًا يَعْبُدُونَنِي لَا يُشْرِكُونَ بِي شَيْئًا وَمَن كَفَرَ بَعْدَ ذَٰلِكَ فَأُولَٰئِكَ هُمُ الْفَاسِقُونَ

Allah has promised those who believe and do good works that He will certainly make them successors in the land as He made those before them to succeed others. And He will establish for them their *din*, which He has approved for them, and will give them in exchange safety after their fear. They serve Me, and do not associate partners with Me. Those who disbelieve, henceforth, they have deviated.

24/55

48.

وَنُرِيدُ أَن نَّمُنَّ عَلَى الَّذِينَ اسْتُضْعِفُوا فِي الْأَرْضِ وَنَجْعَلَهُمْ أَئِمَّةً وَنَجْعَلَهُمُ الْوَارِثِينَ

We desired to show kindness to those who were oppressed in the land and to make them leaders and to make them inheritors.

28/5

49.

أَلَا إِنَّ أَوْلِيَاءَ اللَّهِ لَا خَوْفٌ عَلَيْهِمْ وَلَا هُمْ يَحْزَنُونَ

Indeed, truly the friends of Allah do not fear, nor do they grieve.

10/62

The just and qualified leaders in this world are those who have groomed the lower self and transcended by guidance of the One Heavenly Leader.

The true lovers of Allah follow the path of eternal joy and happiness; they do not succumb to worldly attachments and disappointments. The nature of this world is uncertainty and affliction whilst the spirit seeks the abode of permanent joy and happiness.

Allah declares His presence and responds to the sincere caller. The awakened seeker restricts his plea to Allah only.

An evil action will bring about its equal and opposite reaction, whereas a virtuous deed will multiply many times. No thought, intention or action will pass without its impact and influence. Each being is the author of his book of records, which will be read and lived accordingly in the Hereafter. There is no escape from what we earn..

50.

هُوَ الَّذِي يُصَلِّي عَلَيْكُمْ وَمَلَائِكَتُهُ لِيُخْرِجَكُم مِّنَ الظُّلُمَاتِ إِلَى النُّورِ وَكَانَ بِالْمُؤْمِنِينَ رَحِيمًا

He it is who blesses you and so do His angels, in order that He may bring you out of darkness into light; and He is Merciful to the believers.

33/43

51.

وَإِذَا سَأَلَكَ عِبَادِي عَنِّي فَإِنِّي قَرِيبٌ أُجِيبُ دَعْوَةَ الدَّاعِ إِذَا دَعَانِ فَلْيَسْتَجِيبُوا لِي وَلْيُؤْمِنُوا بِي لَعَلَّهُمْ يَرْشُدُونَ

And when My servant asks you about Me, surely I am near. I answer the prayer of the supplicant when he calls Me. Therefore, they should respond to Me and have faith in Me in order that they may be rightly guided.

2/186

52.

مَن جَاءَ بِالْحَسَنَةِ فَلَهُ عَشْرُ أَمْثَالِهَا وَمَن جَاءَ بِالسَّيِّئَةِ فَلَا يُجْزَىٰ إِلَّا مِثْلَهَا وَهُمْ لَا يُظْلَمُونَ

Those who produce a good deed will receive tenfold like it, while those who bring an evil deed will only be compensated for the like of it, and they will not be wronged.

6/160

53.

وَإِذْ تَأَذَّنَ رَبُّكُمْ لَئِن شَكَرْتُمْ لَأَزِيدَنَّكُمْ وَلَئِن كَفَرْتُمْ إِنَّ عَذَابِي لَشَدِيدٌ

And when your Lord proclaimed: If you give thanks, I will give you more; but if you are thankless, then my punishment is severe.

14/7

54.

$$\text{وَكُلُّ شَيْءٍ فَعَلُوهُ فِي الزُّبُرِ}$$
$$\text{وَكُلُّ صَغِيرٍ وَكَبِيرٍ مُّسْتَطَرٌ}$$

And everything they did is in the Writing. And every small and large thing is recorded.

54/52-53

55.

$$\text{تِلْكَ أُمَّةٌ قَدْ خَلَتْ ۖ لَهَا مَا كَسَبَتْ وَلَكُم مَّا كَسَبْتُمْ ۖ وَلَا تُسْأَلُونَ عَمَّا كَانُوا يَعْمَلُونَ}$$

That was a community, which has long since passed away. It has what it earned and you have what you have earned. You will not be questioned about what they did.

2/134

As every individual is accountable, so are societies and nations. These are dynamic relationships between the human being and the prevailing culture and society.

CHAPTER FOUR

ALLAH'S COMMANDS

Allah created time and space as a confined arena, for the spirits and souls of the family of Adam. All aspects of life are experienced as cause and effect, one leading into the other. Today is yesterday's child and the mother of tomorrow.

Allah's commands are the naturally intended direction of creation within the time-space dimension. By following these commands we are free of the many veils of misconception, deception and frustration. If we desire a life of grace with the least amount of personal and social affliction then we must act according to Divine intention and design. The sincere seeker is in a state of constant self-awareness, accountability, humility, and realization of the nearness of death and the ongoingness of life hereafter.

In a revealed tradition (*hadith qudsi*) Allah says: 'I was a hidden treasure and I loved to be known'. This condition can only be realized if one takes on higher attributes and sublimates the lower human tendencies. Allah has created human beings with lower tendencies so that they may maintain humility and take refuge in His mercy, forgiveness and perfection.

The sincere seeker is honest, forthright, and clearly sees his urgent need for spiritual growth and awakening. Thus he considers the Qur'anic verses, especially Allah's commands and prohibitions, as directed primarily to himself.

The goal of creation is balance. For the human being balance means inner contentment which is true happiness, not happiness based on outward fleeting satisfactions. The driving forces to achieve stability and contentment are the energies of attraction towards what is liked and repulsion away from what is disliked. If the self, however, is not educated and groomed so that these two energies are refined towards the higher aspects of the self, the individual will be left pandering to his or her lower desires. Allah's commands and prohibitions relate to this grooming of the self so that the highest potential - the spirit within - is illumined.

1.

يَا أَيُّهَا الَّذِينَ آمَنُوا اسْتَجِيبُوا لِلَّهِ وَلِلرَّسُولِ إِذَا دَعَاكُمْ لِمَا يُحْيِيكُمْ وَاعْلَمُوا أَنَّ اللَّهَ يَحُولُ بَيْنَ الْمَرْءِ وَقَلْبِهِ وَأَنَّهُ إِلَيْهِ تُحْشَرُونَ

O you who believe, obey Allah and the messenger when He calls you to that which brings you life, and know that Allah comes in between a being and his own heart, and that to Him you will be gathered.

8/24

The ultimate purpose of life is to know the truth behind existence, the meaning of death and the subsequent eternal life. This is knowledge of Allah.

2.

وَسَارِعُوا إِلَىٰ مَغْفِرَةٍ مِّن رَّبِّكُمْ وَجَنَّةٍ عَرْضُهَا السَّمَاوَاتُ وَالْأَرْضُ أُعِدَّتْ لِلْمُتَّقِينَ

And hasten forth in the way that leads to forgiveness from your Lord, and Paradise as wide as the heavens and the earth, prepared for those who are cautiously aware.

3/133

3.

يَا أَيُّهَا الَّذِينَ آمَنُوا تُوبُوا إِلَى اللَّهِ تَوْبَةً نَّصُوحًا عَسَىٰ رَبُّكُمْ أَن يُكَفِّرَ عَنكُمْ سَيِّئَاتِكُمْ وَيُدْخِلَكُمْ جَنَّاتٍ تَجْرِي مِن تَحْتِهَا الْأَنْهَارُ يَوْمَ لَا يُخْزِي اللَّهُ النَّبِيَّ وَالَّذِينَ آمَنُوا مَعَهُ نُورُهُمْ يَسْعَىٰ بَيْنَ أَيْدِيهِمْ وَبِأَيْمَانِهِمْ يَقُولُونَ رَبَّنَا أَتْمِمْ لَنَا نُورَنَا وَاغْفِرْ لَنَا إِنَّكَ عَلَىٰ كُلِّ شَيْءٍ قَدِيرٌ

O, you who believe turn to Allah in sincere repentance. It may be that your Lord will remit from your sins and bring you into Gardens under which rivers flow. (This is) a day when Allah will not disgrace the Prophet and those who believe with him. Their light will run before them and on their right hands. They will say: Our Lord, Perfect our Light for us and grant us forgiveness! Indeed, You are able to do all things.

66/8

The ultimate paradise is beyond physical measures and the cage of time and space. In this life, however, we experience aspects of both the garden and hell in preparation for the appropriate abode in the Hereafter. The prescription for this journey is avoidance of falsehood and evils and the constant striving for the perfection of truth and virtuous qualities.

To turn to Him is to be guided by His Light towards the knowledge of His supreme Perfection and Glory. This depends on sincere selfless actions, submission, and constant awareness of His presence.

While preparing the self for departure, the seeker does not deny this world, for all that we experience here is a prelude to and example of the unseen worlds.

Patience is the foundation for illumined reflection. It is the door to the courtyard of knowledge and insight.

Generosity and giving to the needy opens the experience of His channels of boundless generosity and gifts.

4.

مَنْ عَمِلَ صَالِحًا مِن ذَكَرٍ أَوْ أُنثَىٰ وَهُوَ مُؤْمِنٌ فَلَنُحْيِيَنَّهُ حَيَاةً طَيِّبَةً ۖ وَلَنَجْزِيَنَّهُمْ أَجْرَهُم بِأَحْسَنِ مَا كَانُوا يَعْمَلُونَ

Whosoever acts correctly, whether male or female, and is a believer, We will certainly make a good life for him or her, and We will certainly recompense them according to the best of what they did.

16/97

5.

وَابْتَغِ فِيمَا آتَاكَ اللَّهُ الدَّارَ الْآخِرَةَ ۖ وَلَا تَنسَ نَصِيبَكَ مِنَ الدُّنْيَا ۖ وَأَحْسِن كَمَا أَحْسَنَ اللَّهُ إِلَيْكَ ۖ وَلَا تَبْغِ الْفَسَادَ فِي الْأَرْضِ ۖ إِنَّ اللَّهَ لَا يُحِبُّ الْمُفْسِدِينَ

And seek the abode of the Hereafter in that which Allah has given you, and do not neglect your portion of the world. Seek to be excellent as Allah has given what is most excellent to you, and do not seek corruption in the earth, Indeed, Allah does not love those who do wrong.

28/77

6.

وَاصْبِرْ لِحُكْمِ رَبِّكَ فَإِنَّكَ بِأَعْيُنِنَا ۖ وَسَبِّحْ بِحَمْدِ رَبِّكَ حِينَ تَقُومُ وَمِنَ اللَّيْلِ فَسَبِّحْهُ وَإِدْبَارَ النُّجُومِ

Be patient for your Lord's judgment, for surely you are in Our sight. And glorify your Lord with praise when you rise. And in the night glorify Him at the setting of the stars.

52/48-49

7.

قَوْلٌ مَّعْرُوفٌ وَمَغْفِرَةٌ خَيْرٌ مِّن صَدَقَةٍ يَتْبَعُهَا أَذًى ۗ وَاللَّهُ غَنِيٌّ حَلِيمٌ

A kind word of forgiveness is better than almsgiving followed by injury. Allah is Self-Sufficient, the Forbearing.

2/263

8.

يَـٰٓأَيُّهَا ٱلَّذِينَ ءَامَنُوٓا۟ أَنفِقُوا۟ مِمَّا رَزَقْنَـٰكُم مِّن قَبْلِ أَن يَأْتِىَ يَوْمٌ لَّا بَيْعٌ فِيهِ وَلَا خُلَّةٌ وَلَا شَفَـٰعَةٌ وَٱلْكَـٰفِرُونَ هُمُ ٱلظَّـٰلِمُونَ

O you who believe, spend of that which We have provided you before a day comes when there will be no trading, nor friendship, nor intercession. The unbelievers are those who obscure the truth.

2/254

A pure heart holds no hatred for anyone, not even for an enemy. It reflects His light of tolerance and understanding. A pure heart is the abode of the soul, which sustains all the perfect divine attributes and qualities.

9.

وَلَا تَسْتَوِى ٱلْحَسَنَةُ وَلَا ٱلسَّيِّئَةُ ٱدْفَعْ بِٱلَّتِى هِىَ أَحْسَنُ فَإِذَا ٱلَّذِى بَيْنَكَ وَبَيْنَهُ عَدَاوَةٌ كَأَنَّهُۥ وَلِىٌّ حَمِيمٌ

The good deed and the bad deed are not alike. Repel the bad deed with one that is better, and then he, between whom and you there was enmity, will be as if he was a warm friend.

41/34

10.

فَٱذْكُرُونِىٓ أَذْكُرْكُمْ وَٱشْكُرُوا۟ لِى وَلَا تَكْفُرُونِ

Therefore remember Me; I will remember you. Give thanks to Me, and do not be ungrateful to Me.

2/152

11.

إِن يَنصُرْكُمُ ٱللَّهُ فَلَا غَالِبَ لَكُمْ وَإِن يَخْذُلْكُمْ فَمَن ذَا ٱلَّذِى يَنصُرُكُم مِّنۢ بَعْدِهِۦ وَعَلَى ٱللَّهِ فَلْيَتَوَكَّلِ ٱلْمُؤْمِنُونَ

If Allah helps you, none can overcome you, and if He withdraws His help from you, who is there who can help you? Upon Allah let the believers depend.

3/160

Remembering Him always takes us away from the ever-changing world of uncertainties and afflictions. His Truth acts as a stabilizing reference point. Success is the extent of our dependence on His ever present perfection.

12.

ادْعُ إِلَىٰ سَبِيلِ رَبِّكَ بِٱلْحِكْمَةِ وَٱلْمَوْعِظَةِ ٱلْحَسَنَةِ وَجَٰدِلْهُم بِٱلَّتِى هِىَ أَحْسَنُ إِنَّ رَبَّكَ هُوَ أَعْلَمُ بِمَن ضَلَّ عَن سَبِيلِهِۦ وَهُوَ أَعْلَمُ بِٱلْمُهْتَدِينَ

Call to the way of the Lord with wisdom and fair counsel, and reason with them in the best possible way. Indeed, your Lord knows best whoever strayed from His way, and He is the one who knows best those who are guided.

16/125

Realize that it is His power behind all existences and experiences. Beg Him for an agreeable destiny while being focused on His ever-presence.

13.

سَمَّٰعُونَ لِلْكَذِبِ أَكَّٰلُونَ لِلسُّحْتِ فَإِن جَآءُوكَ فَٱحْكُم بَيْنَهُمْ أَوْ أَعْرِضْ عَنْهُمْ وَإِن تُعْرِضْ عَنْهُمْ فَلَن يَضُرُّوكَ شَيْـًٔا وَإِنْ حَكَمْتَ فَٱحْكُم بَيْنَهُم بِٱلْقِسْطِ إِنَّ ٱللَّهَ يُحِبُّ ٱلْمُقْسِطِينَ

Listeners to lies and consumers of illicit gains! If they come to you, judge between them or turn away from them. If you turn away from them, then they cannot harm you at all. But if you judge, judge between them with equity. Indeed, Allah loves the equitable.

5/42

Be just and equitable always. Remember His justice and mercy. Do not forget His Might and power of Compulsion and Majesty. Be in constant gratitude and in obedience to the natural laws that are His - the way of life.

14.

وَٱذْكُرُوا۟ نِعْمَةَ ٱللَّهِ عَلَيْكُمْ وَمِيثَٰقَهُ ٱلَّذِى وَاثَقَكُم بِهِۦ إِذْ قُلْتُمْ سَمِعْنَا وَأَطَعْنَا وَٱتَّقُوا۟ ٱللَّهَ إِنَّ ٱللَّهَ عَلِيمٌۢ بِذَاتِ ٱلصُّدُورِ

Remember Allah's favour upon you and His covenant with which He bound you when you said: We hear and we obey; and we have cautious awareness of Allah. Surely, Allah knows the innermost of hearts.

5/7

Do not act lavishly or meanly - be considerate, moderate, equitable and in cautious awareness. He sees and knows all.

15.

وَلَا تَجْعَلْ يَدَكَ مَغْلُولَةً إِلَىٰ عُنُقِكَ وَلَا تَبْسُطْهَا كُلَّ الْبَسْطِ فَتَقْعُدَ مَلُومًا مَّحْسُورًا ۝ إِنَّ رَبَّكَ يَبْسُطُ الرِّزْقَ لِمَن يَشَاءُ وَيَقْدِرُ ۚ إِنَّهُ كَانَ بِعِبَادِهِ خَبِيرًا بَصِيرًا

Do not keep your hand chained to your neck, nor stretch it to its full extent so that you become worthy of blame and destitute. Indeed, your Lord makes provision plentiful and restricts it for whomever He pleases. Surely, He is Ever - Aware, and the one who sees his servant.

17/29-30

Be patient as He is with you. Counsel others, and go forth while depending upon Him.

16.

فَبِمَا رَحْمَةٍ مِّنَ اللَّهِ لِنتَ لَهُمْ ۖ وَلَوْ كُنتَ فَظًّا غَلِيظَ الْقَلْبِ لَانفَضُّوا مِنْ حَوْلِكَ ۖ فَاعْفُ عَنْهُمْ وَاسْتَغْفِرْ لَهُمْ وَشَاوِرْهُمْ فِي الْأَمْرِ ۖ فَإِذَا عَزَمْتَ فَتَوَكَّلْ عَلَى اللَّهِ ۚ إِنَّ اللَّهَ يُحِبُّ الْمُتَوَكِّلِينَ

It was by the mercy of Allah that you were lenient with them, for if you had been stern and hard hearted, they would certainly have left you. So pardon them and ask forgiveness for them, and consult with them about affairs. When you have resolved which course to take, place your trust completely in Allah. Surely, Allah loves those who are in full trust.

3/159

Persevere during adversity with patient determination and reliance upon Him

17.

وَكَأَيِّن مِّن نَّبِيٍّ قَاتَلَ مَعَهُ رِبِّيُّونَ كَثِيرٌ فَمَا وَهَنُوا لِمَا أَصَابَهُمْ فِي سَبِيلِ اللَّهِ وَمَا ضَعُفُوا وَمَا اسْتَكَانُوا ۗ وَاللَّهُ يُحِبُّ الصَّابِرِينَ

And how many of the prophets fought (in Allah's way) and with them were many pious ones? But they never lost heart if they met with disaster in Allah's way, nor did they weaken nor give in. And Allah loves those firm and steadfast.

3/146

Strive, struggle and fight in His way with all you have. The universe belongs to Him. We are only His guests, sustained by Him to witness, adore and worship Him.

> Creation is weak and in need of Him. We are from Him and to Him we return; therefore, we must reflect His great Attributes and Qualities.

18.

لَا يَسْتَوِي الْقَاعِدُونَ مِنَ الْمُؤْمِنِينَ غَيْرُ أُولِي الضَّرَرِ وَالْمُجَاهِدُونَ فِي سَبِيلِ اللَّهِ بِأَمْوَالِهِمْ وَأَنفُسِهِمْ فَضَّلَ اللَّهُ الْمُجَاهِدِينَ بِأَمْوَالِهِمْ وَأَنفُسِهِمْ عَلَى الْقَاعِدِينَ دَرَجَةً وَكُلًّا وَعَدَ اللَّهُ الْحُسْنَىٰ وَفَضَّلَ اللَّهُ الْمُجَاهِدِينَ عَلَى الْقَاعِدِينَ أَجْرًا عَظِيمًا

Those of the believers that stay behind, other than those who are disabled, are not the same as those who strive in the way of Allah with their property and lives. Allah has given a higher rank to those who strive with their property and lives than those who stay behind. Allah has promised the best to all, but He prefers those who strive above those who are sedentary.

4/95

19.

هَا أَنتُمْ هَٰؤُلَاءِ تُدْعَوْنَ لِتُنفِقُوا فِي سَبِيلِ اللَّهِ فَمِنكُم مَّن يَبْخَلُ وَمَن يَبْخَلْ فَإِنَّمَا يَبْخَلُ عَن نَّفْسِهِ وَاللَّهُ الْغَنِيُّ وَأَنتُمُ الْفُقَرَاءُ وَإِن تَتَوَلَّوْا يَسْتَبْدِلْ قَوْمًا غَيْرَكُمْ ثُمَّ لَا يَكُونُوا أَمْثَالَكُم

Indeed, here you are, those who are called upon to spend in the way of Allah, yet among you are those who withhold. And as for he who withholds, his stinginess is against himself. And Allah is the Self-sufficient, and you are the poor. And if you turn back, he will bring another people in your place, and they will not be like you

47/38

20.

قُلْ سِيرُوا فِي الْأَرْضِ فَانظُرُوا كَيْفَ كَانَ عَاقِبَةُ الَّذِينَ مِن قَبْلُ ۚ كَانَ أَكْثَرُهُم مُّشْرِكِينَ

Say: Travel in the land, and see what the end was of those who were before you. Most of them associated partners with Allah.

30/42

Travel in the land and reflect. Where are they now? What is their reward?

21.

أَفَلَمْ يَسِيرُوا فِي الْأَرْضِ فَتَكُونَ لَهُمْ قُلُوبٌ يَعْقِلُونَ بِهَا أَوْ آذَانٌ يَسْمَعُونَ بِهَا ۖ فَإِنَّهَا لَا تَعْمَى الْأَبْصَارُ وَلَٰكِن تَعْمَى الْقُلُوبُ الَّتِي فِي الصُّدُورِ

Have they not traveled in the land so that they have hearts with which to understand or ears with which to hear? For indeed it is not the eyes that are blind, but it is the hearts in the breasts that are blind.

22/46

It is through the purified heart that you gain insight and enlightenment.

22.

وَإِذْ نَتَقْنَا الْجَبَلَ فَوْقَهُمْ كَأَنَّهُ ظُلَّةٌ وَظَنُّوا أَنَّهُ وَاقِعٌ بِهِمْ خُذُوا مَا آتَيْنَاكُم بِقُوَّةٍ وَاذْكُرُوا مَا فِيهِ لَعَلَّكُمْ تَتَّقُونَ

And when We shook the mountain over them as if it were a covering overhead, and they thought that it was going to fall down upon them: Take hold of what We have given you with firmness, and be mindful of what is in it, so that you may guard (against evil).

7/171

Listen with your heart and be illumined. There is outer sight, insight, and above all, His Light, which is in the core of a purified heart. Stick to that which you know is true.

Courtesy is to enter through the correct door in every situation. Failure and confusion are due to ignorance of the appropriate keys for the particular door. Courtesy is based on applying the proper mode or skill, to the situation at hand. This leads to success.

The world is disturbed when we transact unjustly and against the nature of things. Examples of this are usury and other tricky ways of dominance and control. This path of agitation will only lead to fire and destruction for all involved.

23.

وَلَيْسَ ٱلْبِرُّ بِأَن تَأْتُوا۟ ٱلْبُيُوتَ مِن ظُهُورِهَا وَلَـٰكِنَّ ٱلْبِرَّ مَنِ ٱتَّقَىٰ وَأْتُوا۟ ٱلْبُيُوتَ مِنْ أَبْوَابِهَا وَٱتَّقُوا۟ ٱللَّهَ لَعَلَّكُمْ تُفْلِحُونَ

...It is not righteous that you enter houses from the rear. But he is righteous who is in cautious awareness. So go into houses through their doors. Be cautiously aware so that you may be successful.

2/189

24.

ٱلَّذِينَ يَأْكُلُونَ ٱلرِّبَا لَا يَقُومُونَ إِلَّا كَمَا يَقُومُ ٱلَّذِي يَتَخَبَّطُهُ ٱلشَّيْطَانُ مِنَ ٱلْمَسِّ ذَٰلِكَ بِأَنَّهُمْ قَالُوٓا۟ إِنَّمَا ٱلْبَيْعُ مِثْلُ ٱلرِّبَا وَأَحَلَّ ٱللَّهُ ٱلْبَيْعَ وَحَرَّمَ ٱلرِّبَا فَمَن جَآءَهُۥ مَوْعِظَةٌ مِّن رَّبِّهِۦ فَٱنتَهَىٰ فَلَهُۥ مَا سَلَفَ وَأَمْرُهُۥٓ إِلَى ٱللَّهِ وَمَنْ عَادَ فَأُو۟لَـٰٓئِكَ أَصْحَابُ ٱلنَّارِ هُمْ فِيهَا خَـٰلِدُونَ

Those who consume usury do not rise except as someone overcome by shaytān's touch. This is because they say: Trade is just like usury. Whereas Allah has permitted trading, he has forbidden usury. So whoever has received a warning from his Lord and then desists, he shall have that which is past, and whoever returns (to usury), such are the companions of the fire. In it they will dwell perpetually.

2/275

CHAPTER FIVE

ALLAH'S PROHIBITIONS

The path of Divine Unity (*tawhīd*) and witnessing the One Absolute Cause is the purpose of all spiritual pursuits. All life's experiences are caused by One Source that manifests countless varieties. The fundamental veil and barrier of unawareness which obscures the ever-present One Divine Light is the illusion of otherness (*shirk*). Being caught with duality and association with Allah our mind and intellect discern cause and effect but remain trapped within this confinement. Seeing other than Him and denying the truth (*kufr*) are the ultimate prohibitions.

The sincere seeker and believer in Allah will navigate in the direction of life's purpose using the rudders of negation and affirmation - negating what is not conducive and affirming positive activities. Falling into the pitfalls of the self and succumbing to its undesirable qualities will only delay and confuse the seeker.

Allah in His infinite Mercy has placed within the primal human imprint the capacity of intellect and cognition to evaluate and acknowledge appropriate deeds and to discard useless distractions. The Qur'an and the prophetic path give us details of what is to be avoided and the appropriate boundaries along the path of submission (*Islam*).

Success along this path is commensurate to the extent of serious yearning and honest endeavour in following its direction. Knowing the clear boundaries, and possessing personal ethics, commitment, faith and steadfastness are essential foundations for spiritual growth.

Allah's mercy and generosity cover every human frailty and fault. To perceive other than Him as the source and essence behind life is a basic flaw that has no cure. He is behind and within all creation. The foundation of the entire cosmos is His unique Light.

1.

إِنَّ اللَّهَ لَا يَغْفِرُ أَن يُشْرَكَ بِهِ وَيَغْفِرُ مَا دُونَ ذَٰلِكَ لِمَن يَشَاءُ وَمَن يُشْرِكْ بِاللَّهِ فَقَدِ افْتَرَىٰ إِثْمًا عَظِيمًا

Certainly Allah does not forgive the association of partners with Him *(shirk)*, whereas He forgives all besides that to whom He pleases. Whoever associates partners with Him has indeed assumed a tremendous sin.

4/48

2.

أَفَأَمِنُوا مَكْرَ اللَّهِ فَلَا يَأْمَنُ مَكْرَ اللَّهِ إِلَّا الْقَوْمُ الْخَاسِرُونَ

Do they feel secure from Allah's plot? None except the people of loss feel secure from Allah's plot.

7/99

3.

وَاللَّهُ لَا يَهْدِي الْقَوْمَ الظَّالِمِينَ

...Allah does not guide people who obscure (truth).

2/258

وَاللَّهُ لَا يَهْدِي الْقَوْمَ الْفَاسِقِينَ

...Allah does not guide people who have deviated from the right course.

5/108

إِنَّ اللَّهَ لَا يَهْدِي مَنْ هُوَ مُسْرِفٌ كَذَّابٌ

...Allah does not guide him who is extravagant, a liar.

40/28

With sincerity, honesty, modesty, courage, wisdom and justice, illumined guidance will follow. This will lead one to better action that in turn will result in deeper knowledge.

4.

$$\text{يَا أَيُّهَا الَّذِينَ آمَنُوا لَا تُبْطِلُوا صَدَقَاتِكُم بِالْمَنِّ وَالْأَذَىٰ كَالَّذِي يُنفِقُ مَالَهُ رِئَاءَ النَّاسِ وَلَا يُؤْمِنُ بِاللَّهِ وَالْيَوْمِ الْآخِرِ ۖ فَمَثَلُهُ كَمَثَلِ صَفْوَانٍ عَلَيْهِ تُرَابٌ فَأَصَابَهُ وَابِلٌ فَتَرَكَهُ صَلْدًا ۖ لَا يَقْدِرُونَ عَلَىٰ شَيْءٍ مِّمَّا كَسَبُوا ۗ وَاللَّهُ لَا يَهْدِي الْقَوْمَ الْكَافِرِينَ}$$

O, You who believe! Do not nullify your charitable works by reminders of your generosity or by injury, like one that spends his wealth showing off to people and not believing in Allah and the Last Day. His likeness is like that of a rock with earth upon it: heavy rain falls on it leaving it bare. They have no control of anything that they have earned. Allah does not guide the people who cover up reality.

2/264

The righteous ones uphold truth at all levels and are watchful of wrong actions that distract them from heightened awareness and insight.

5.

$$\text{وَأَمَّا الَّذِينَ آمَنُوا وَعَمِلُوا الصَّالِحَاتِ فَيُوَفِّيهِمْ أُجُورَهُمْ ۗ وَاللَّهُ لَا يُحِبُّ الظَّالِمِينَ}$$

As for those who believe and act correctly, Allah will recompense them fully; but Allah does not love those who obscure truth and oppress.

3/57

$$\text{قُلْ أَطِيعُوا اللَّهَ وَالرَّسُولَ ۖ فَإِن تَوَلَّوْا فَإِنَّ اللَّهَ لَا يُحِبُّ الْكَافِرِينَ}$$

Say: Obey Allah and His messenger. But if they turn away, Allah does not love those who cover up reality.

3/32

Allah has designed mankind such that we strive towards His perfection. Thus He shuns those who are unjust to themselves and deny His Supreme Perfection. This lack of yearning and striving brings about corruption and transgression. He abhors arrogance, disloyalty, meanness, covetousness, oppression and all other injurious qualities.

The path is founded on grooming the self and curbing all lower tendencies keeping within the natural boundaries, as revealed to the prophets.

Allah loves the virtuous beings that make the ego subservient to the soul, which is humble to its Lord and contains His attributes and qualities.

وَاللَّهُ لَا يُحِبُّ كُلَّ كَفَّارٍ أَثِيمٍ

...Allah does not love those who disbelieve, acting impiously.

2/276

وَاللَّهُ لَا يُحِبُّ الْمُفْسِدِينَ

...Allah does not love those who are corrupt and unsound.

5/64

إِنَّ اللَّهَ لَا يُحِبُّ الْمُعْتَدِينَ

...Allah does not love those who transgress the bounds.

5/87

إِنَّ اللَّهَ لَا يُحِبُّ الْخَائِنِينَ

...Allah does not love those who are false, disloyal, and treacherous.

8/58

يَا بَنِي آدَمَ خُذُوا زِينَتَكُمْ عِندَ كُلِّ مَسْجِدٍ وَكُلُوا وَاشْرَبُوا وَلَا تُسْرِفُوا إِنَّهُ لَا يُحِبُّ الْمُسْرِفِينَ

O Children of Adam, attend to your adornment at every time of prayer and eat and drink, but be not excessive. Indeed, He likes not those who commit excess.

7/31

إِنَّ اللَّهَ لَا يُحِبُّ كُلَّ مُخْتَالٍ فَخُورٍ

Allah does not love the self-conceited boaster

31/18

6.

$$\text{الَّذِينَ يُجَادِلُونَ فِي آيَاتِ اللَّهِ بِغَيْرِ سُلْطَانٍ أَتَاهُمْ كَبُرَ مَقْتًا عِندَ اللَّهِ وَعِندَ الَّذِينَ آمَنُوا كَذَٰلِكَ يَطْبَعُ اللَّهُ عَلَىٰ كُلِّ قَلْبِ مُتَكَبِّرٍ جَبَّارٍ}$$

Those who dispute concerning the revelations of Allah without any authority that has come to them, (do that which) is greatly disliked by Allah and those who believe. Thus does Allah seal up the heart of everyone who thinks himself great and mighty.

40/35

Outer trouble and turmoil are clear signs and symptoms of inner sickness, calling for remedial intentions and appropriate actions

7.

$$\text{وَمَن يَعْشُ عَن ذِكْرِ الرَّحْمَٰنِ نُقَيِّضْ لَهُ شَيْطَانًا فَهُوَ لَهُ قَرِينٌ}$$

And whoever turns himself away from the remembrance of the Beneficent, We assign to him a devil that becomes his companion.

43/36

8.

$$\text{ظَهَرَ الْفَسَادُ فِي الْبَرِّ وَالْبَحْرِ بِمَا كَسَبَتْ أَيْدِي النَّاسِ لِيُذِيقَهُم بَعْضَ الَّذِي عَمِلُوا لَعَلَّهُمْ يَرْجِعُونَ}$$

Corruption has appeared on the land and in the sea because of what people have earned, that He may make them taste a part of that which they have done, so that they may return.

30/41

It is His mercy that is behind human suffering and afflictions due to wrong actions and neglect of the original purpose of life. In all cases, confusion, discord and turmoil are signs of transgression and deviation from the prophetic path, of self-knowledge and awakening to the higher zone of consciousness within.

There is no option but to submit to His Design and Will and to return to Him with humbleness, repentance and readiness for success in this world and the next.

The time to experience contentment is the present moment. The past is gone and the future is uncertain and only partially in our hands. The only certainty is now.

The sincere seeker has no option but to struggle both outwardly and inwardly in the way of truth and justice while relying increasingly upon His Guidance and Light.

9.

مُنِيبِينَ إِلَيْهِ وَاتَّقُوهُ وَأَقِيمُوا الصَّلَاةَ وَلَا تَكُونُوا مِنَ الْمُشْرِكِينَ مِنَ الَّذِينَ فَرَّقُوا دِينَهُمْ وَكَانُوا شِيَعًا ۖ كُلُّ حِزْبٍ بِمَا لَدَيْهِمْ فَرِحُونَ

Turn to Him and be cautiously aware of Him; and establish worship and be not of those who associate partners with Allah. Of those who split up their religion (dīn) and form sects, each faction rejoices in what they have.

30/31-32

10.

لِكَيْلَا تَأْسَوْا عَلَىٰ مَا فَاتَكُمْ وَلَا تَفْرَحُوا بِمَا آتَاكُمْ ۗ وَاللَّهُ لَا يُحِبُّ كُلَّ مُخْتَالٍ فَخُورٍ

In order that you may not grieve over what has passed you by, nor rejoice for that which has been given to you. Allah does not love those who are fancifully deluded and proud

57/23

11.

وَقَاتِلُوا فِي سَبِيلِ اللَّهِ الَّذِينَ يُقَاتِلُونَكُمْ وَلَا تَعْتَدُوا ۚ إِنَّ اللَّهَ لَا يُحِبُّ الْمُعْتَدِينَ

Fight in the way of Allah against those who fight against you, but do not go beyond the limits. Surely, Allah does not love the aggressors.

2/190

12.

يَا أَيُّهَا الَّذِينَ آمَنُوا اجْتَنِبُوا كَثِيرًا مِنَ الظَّنِّ إِنَّ بَعْضَ الظَّنِّ إِثْمٌ وَلَا تَجَسَّسُوا وَلَا يَغْتَبْ بَعْضُكُمْ بَعْضًا أَيُحِبُّ أَحَدُكُمْ أَنْ يَأْكُلَ لَحْمَ أَخِيهِ مَيْتًا فَكَرِهْتُمُوهُ وَاتَّقُوا اللَّهَ إِنَّ اللَّهَ تَوَّابٌ رَحِيمٌ

O you who believe, avoid most suspicion; indeed, some suspicion is a misdeed. Do not spy and do not backbite one another. Would one of you like to eat the flesh of his dead brother? You would dislike it intensely. Have cautious awareness of Allah. Indeed, Allah is Forgiving and Merciful.

49/12

The seekers with faith and trust follow a narrow path of conduct in the world of change and turmoil. They avoid all evils and act with compassion and good intentions for all of creation.

13.

يَمْحَقُ اللَّهُ الرِّبَا وَيُرْبِي الصَّدَقَاتِ وَاللَّهُ لَا يُحِبُّ كُلَّ كَفَّارٍ أَثِيمٍ

Allah will obliterate usury *(riba)* and will make acts of charity *(sadaqa)* grow. Allah does not love those who disbelieve and are impious

2/276

Usury is a great destroyer of trust and cohesion in society. It causes injustice and misery being founded on the love of this world and supremacy of material wealth at the cost of corruption and abuse.

14.

وَآمِنُوا بِمَا أَنْزَلْتُ مُصَدِّقًا لِمَا مَعَكُمْ وَلَا تَكُونُوا أَوَّلَ كَافِرٍ بِهِ وَلَا تَشْتَرُوا بِآيَاتِي ثَمَنًا قَلِيلًا وَإِيَّايَ فَاتَّقُونِ

Have faith *(imān)* in what I have sent down confirming what is with you, and do not be quick to reject it. Do not exchange My signs for a paltry price and have constant awareness of Me alone.

2/41

The ultimate hypocrisy is to preach to others without applying it to oneself. One is then veiled from His ever-present witnessing and knowledge.

The religion (dīn) is the code of life and enlightenment for the serious believers in the constancy of Divine Presence and Lordship. The path has to be lived fully in order to realize and witness His glory and be free from the veils of the self. The ultimate fruit of enlightenment is seeing the One Source and origin of all existence and events.

15

أَتَأْمُرُونَ النَّاسَ بِالْبِرِّ وَتَنْسَوْنَ أَنْفُسَكُمْ وَأَنْتُمْ تَتْلُونَ الْكِتَابَ أَفَلَا تَعْقِلُونَ

Do you enjoin people to be devout and forget (to be so) yourself while you recite the Book? Have you no intellect? 2/44

16.

يَا أَيُّهَا الَّذِينَ آمَنُوا لِمَ تَقُولُونَ مَا لَا تَفْعَلُونَ كَبُرَ مَقْتًا عِنْدَ اللَّهِ أَنْ تَقُولُوا مَا لَا تَفْعَلُونَ

O you who believe, why do you speak about what you do not do? It is deeply abhorrent to Allah that you should say what you do not do. 61/2-3

17.

يَا أَيُّهَا الَّذِينَ آمَنُوا لَا تَتَّخِذُوا الَّذِينَ اتَّخَذُوا دِينَكُمْ هُزُوًا وَلَعِبًا مِنَ الَّذِينَ أُوتُوا الْكِتَابَ مِنْ قَبْلِكُمْ وَالْكُفَّارَ أَوْلِيَاءَ وَاتَّقُوا اللَّهَ إِنْ كُنْتُمْ مُؤْمِنِينَ

O you who believe! Do not take friends from among those who have contempt for your religion or regard it lightly from among those who received the Book before you and from among the disbelievers. Be in constant awareness of Allah if you are believers.

5/57

CHAPTER SIX

ALLAH'S CREATION

Allah is the Lord of all the worlds. He is the Great, the Mighty, the Merciful, the Creator of the heavens and earth and all that is between them. He is the Creator of human kind and the unseen entities of this world and the Hereafter, good and evil, the fire and the garden, angels, prophets and messengers. From Him everything emanates, by Him everything is sustained and to Him everything returns.

All creation exists in pairs and opposites. All human experiences reflect this reality. There is life and death, light and darkness, good and bad, heaven and earth, knowledge and ignorance, health and illness. Human beings need to discover the ways of nature in order to work alongside its patterns so that harmony may be achieved and maintained. The Qur'an unveils the knowledge of Allah's creational designs and intentions for us to submit to His blueprint and follow His programme.

The physical world is only a portion of the total creation, like the tip of an iceberg. The unseen is far greater than that which appears solid and physical. The Qur'an describes the seven heavens, the earth, angelic powers and energies, as well as the satanic forces.

Our world is primarily experienced and understood through causal dynamics. One action leads to another. Human endeavour is motivated by the desire of happiness, which in turn is a result of contentment and peace. The ultimate human objective is to have a pure heart with living faith, unconditional love of Allah and awakened surrender to His ever-flowing mercy.

The physical and material world, as well as the world of actions and causality, is held together by His unity, which may be perceived by understanding, cognition and witnessing. All discernible realms follow patterns and laws that relate to the dominion of Divine Qualities and Attributes. Allah's perfect qualities operate as subtle unifying beams and threads of energy within creation.

Divine unity in essence is the most subtle and mysterious truth and engulfs all that is discernable as well as what is unknown. All of Allah's creation is dependent on His Light or Essence and is sustained by it and to it all returns.

Allah's Creation

1.

وَمَا خَلَقْتُ الْجِنَّ وَالْإِنسَ إِلَّا لِيَعْبُدُونِ

I have created the invisible entities *(jinn)* and humankind only that they might worship Me.

51/56

2.

إِنَّ فِي خَلْقِ السَّمَاوَاتِ وَالْأَرْضِ وَاخْتِلَافِ اللَّيْلِ وَالنَّهَارِ وَالْفُلْكِ الَّتِي تَجْرِي فِي الْبَحْرِ بِمَا يَنفَعُ النَّاسَ وَمَا أَنزَلَ اللَّهُ مِنَ السَّمَاءِ مِن مَّاءٍ فَأَحْيَا بِهِ الْأَرْضَ بَعْدَ مَوْتِهَا وَبَثَّ فِيهَا مِن كُلِّ دَابَّةٍ وَتَصْرِيفِ الرِّيَاحِ وَالسَّحَابِ الْمُسَخَّرِ بَيْنَ السَّمَاءِ وَالْأَرْضِ لَآيَاتٍ لِّقَوْمٍ يَعْقِلُونَ

Behold! In the creation of the heavens and the earth, and the difference of night and day, and the ships which run upon the sea and that which is of use to men, and the water which Allah sends down from the sky, thereby reviving the earth after it's death, and scattering about in it creatures of every kind, and the changing of the winds, and the clouds subservient between heaven and earth, in all of these are signs (of Allah's sovereignty) for people who understand.

2/164

The purpose of creation is knowledge, adoration and worship of the Creator. The determined seeker will contemplate His perfect ways and how all the diverse creations are connected and interlinked by His Oneness.

All existence emanates from Him, is sustained by Him and returns to Him. He is the Permanent Lord and Master, and His signs are everywhere in His domain.

3

وَمِنْ آيَاتِهِ أَنْ خَلَقَ لَكُم مِّنْ أَنفُسِكُمْ أَزْوَاجًا لِّتَسْكُنُوا إِلَيْهَا وَجَعَلَ بَيْنَكُم مَّوَدَّةً وَرَحْمَةً ۚ إِنَّ فِي ذَٰلِكَ لَآيَاتٍ لِّقَوْمٍ يَتَفَكَّرُونَ وَمِنْ آيَاتِهِ خَلْقُ السَّمَاوَاتِ وَالْأَرْضِ وَاخْتِلَافُ أَلْسِنَتِكُمْ وَأَلْوَانِكُمْ ۚ إِنَّ فِي ذَٰلِكَ لَآيَاتٍ لِّلْعَالِمِينَ

Created things are diverse and contain opposite qualities and attributes. All experiences are related by cause and effect. This world is but a prelude and an indication for the Hereafter. From the One essence emerge duality and plurality as signs and indications of the One.

And among His signs is that He created mates from yourselves, that you may find tranquility in them. And He has placed between you love and compassion. Surely in that are signs for people who reflect. And of His signs is the creation of the heavens and the earth and the diversity of your tongues and colours. Surely, there are signs in that for those who have knowledge.

30/21-22

وَمِنْ آيَاتِهِ يُرِيكُمُ الْبَرْقَ خَوْفًا وَطَمَعًا وَيُنَزِّلُ مِنَ السَّمَاءِ مَاءً فَيُحْيِي بِهِ الْأَرْضَ بَعْدَ مَوْتِهَا ۚ إِنَّ فِي ذَٰلِكَ لَآيَاتٍ لِّقَوْمٍ يَعْقِلُونَ وَمِنْ آيَاتِهِ أَن تَقُومَ السَّمَاءُ وَالْأَرْضُ بِأَمْرِهِ ۚ ثُمَّ إِذَا دَعَاكُمْ دَعْوَةً مِّنَ الْأَرْضِ إِذَا أَنتُمْ تَخْرُجُونَ

His natural signs include all that is in the earth and heavens, in meaning and form.

And of His signs is that He manifests lightning, so that you may fear and hope, and He sends down water from the sky thus giving life to the earth after it's death. Surely there are signs in that for people who understand. And among His signs is that the heavens and earth are sustained by His command. Then, when He calls you from the earth, you will come forth.

30/24-25

Allah's Creation

4.

خَلَقَ السَّمَاوَاتِ وَالْأَرْضَ بِالْحَقِّ يُكَوِّرُ اللَّيْلَ عَلَى النَّهَارِ وَيُكَوِّرُ النَّهَارَ عَلَى اللَّيْلِ وَسَخَّرَ الشَّمْسَ وَالْقَمَرَ كُلٌّ يَجْرِي لِأَجَلٍ مُسَمًّى

He has created the heavens and the earth with truth. He causes the night to follow the day and the day to follow the night, and He has made the sun and the moon subservient, each one following a specified course...

39/5

Within the Time / Space dimension one phase or aspect of existence leads to another. Nothing is ever exactly the same, yet all relates to His attributes and will.

5.

تُسَبِّحُ لَهُ السَّمَاوَاتُ السَّبْعُ وَالْأَرْضُ وَمَن فِيهِنَّ وَإِن مِّن شَيْءٍ إِلَّا يُسَبِّحُ بِحَمْدِهِ وَلَكِن لَّا تَفْقَهُونَ تَسْبِيحَهُمْ إِنَّهُ كَانَ حَلِيمًا غَفُورًا

The seven heavens and the earth and those in them praise Him, and there is nothing that does not glorify Him with praise, but you do not understand their glorification. Truly, He is Forbearing, Forgiving.

17/44

Causality is the foundation of reason and experience. Yet every creation is sustained by its desire and passion for His perfect qualities.

6.

وَتَرَى الْجِبَالَ تَحْسَبُهَا جَامِدَةً وَهِيَ تَمُرُّ مَرَّ السَّحَابِ صُنْعَ اللَّهِ الَّذِي أَتْقَنَ كُلَّ شَيْءٍ إِنَّهُ خَبِيرٌ بِمَا تَفْعَلُونَ

And you will see the mountains that you had thought solid pass away like the passing of clouds. (This is) the design of Allah who perfected all things. Surely he is well aware of what you do.

27/88

The universe appears solid but in fact transient and flimsy if you view it with the eye of timelessness. The heavens and earth were joined together. Then came the separation whereby stars and planets were formed and life on earth evolved upon the foundation of water. All the dispersed and diverse creations are unified in His gatheredness.

The Adamic soul is the highest of all creation, but it was exposed to the deviation known as Shaytān and thus developed self-awareness, ego and the opposing experiences of evil and virtue. This exposure and choice given to Adam is both a challenge and a gift. But it must be understood properly and acted upon according to the innate and original natural direction.

7.

أَوَلَمْ يَرَ الَّذِينَ كَفَرُوا أَنَّ السَّمَاوَاتِ وَالْأَرْضَ كَانَتَا رَتْقًا فَفَتَقْنَاهُمَا وَجَعَلْنَا مِنَ الْمَاءِ كُلَّ شَيْءٍ حَيٍّ أَفَلَا يُؤْمِنُونَ

Have not those who are in denial of truth (*kufr*) known that the heavens and the earth were stitched together (as one piece), and then We rent them apart, and We made every living thing of water. Will they not then have faith (*īmān*)?

21/30

8.

وَلَقَدْ خَلَقْنَاكُمْ ثُمَّ صَوَّرْنَاكُمْ ثُمَّ قُلْنَا لِلْمَلَائِكَةِ اسْجُدُوا لِآدَمَ فَسَجَدُوا إِلَّا إِبْلِيسَ لَمْ يَكُنْ مِنَ السَّاجِدِينَ
قَالَ مَا مَنَعَكَ أَلَّا تَسْجُدَ إِذْ أَمَرْتُكَ قَالَ أَنَا خَيْرٌ مِنْهُ خَلَقْتَنِي مِنْ نَارٍ وَخَلَقْتَهُ مِنْ طِينٍ
قَالَ فَاهْبِطْ مِنْهَا فَمَا يَكُونُ لَكَ أَنْ تَتَكَبَّرَ فِيهَا فَاخْرُجْ إِنَّكَ مِنَ الصَّاغِرِينَ
قَالَ أَنْظِرْنِي إِلَى يَوْمِ يُبْعَثُونَ

And We indeed created you, then fashioned you, Then We said to the angels, "Prostrate to Adam"; so they prostrated, except for Iblīs. He was not of those who prostrated. He (Allah) said: What prevented you from prostrating when I commanded you to? He (Iblīs) said: I am better than he. You created me from fire, and you created him from mud. He (Allah) said: Then descend from heaven. It is not for you to be arrogant here. Go forth, for indeed, you are of those are despised He (Iblīs) said: Grant me reprieve until the day when they are raised (from the dead).

7/11-14

Allah's Creation

9.

ٱلرَّحْمَٰنُ ۝ عَلَّمَ ٱلْقُرْءَانَ ۝ خَلَقَ ٱلْإِنسَٰنَ ۝ عَلَّمَهُ ٱلْبَيَانَ ۝ ٱلشَّمْسُ وَٱلْقَمَرُ بِحُسْبَانٍ ۝ وَٱلنَّجْمُ وَٱلشَّجَرُ يَسْجُدَانِ ۝ وَٱلسَّمَآءَ رَفَعَهَا وَوَضَعَ ٱلْمِيزَانَ ۝ أَلَّا تَطْغَوْاْ فِى ٱلْمِيزَانِ ۝ وَأَقِيمُواْ ٱلْوَزْنَ بِٱلْقِسْطِ وَلَا تُخْسِرُواْ ٱلْمِيزَانَ ۝ وَٱلْأَرْضَ وَضَعَهَا لِلْأَنَامِ ۝ فِيهَا فَٰكِهَةٌ وَٱلنَّخْلُ ذَاتُ ٱلْأَكْمَامِ ۝ وَٱلْحَبُّ ذُو ٱلْعَصْفِ وَٱلرَّيْحَانُ ۝ فَبِأَىِّ ءَالَآءِ رَبِّكُمَا تُكَذِّبَانِ ۝ خَلَقَ ٱلْإِنسَٰنَ مِن صَلْصَٰلٍ كَٱلْفَخَّارِ ۝ وَخَلَقَ ٱلْجَآنَّ مِن مَّارِجٍ مِّن نَّارٍ ۝ فَبِأَىِّ ءَالَآءِ رَبِّكُمَا تُكَذِّبَانِ ۝ رَبُّ ٱلْمَشْرِقَيْنِ وَرَبُّ ٱلْمَغْرِبَيْنِ ۝ فَبِأَىِّ ءَالَآءِ رَبِّكُمَا تُكَذِّبَانِ ۝ مَرَجَ ٱلْبَحْرَيْنِ يَلْتَقِيَانِ ۝ بَيْنَهُمَا بَرْزَخٌ لَّا يَبْغِيَانِ ۝

The All - Merciful Who taught the Qur'an He created man, And He taught him (clear) expression. The sun and the moon move with precision. The herbs and the trees bow down in prostration. And the sky He uplifted and He established the balanced universal laws, So that you would not exceed this balance, so establish the balance with equity and do not fall short in the measure. The earth he has laid out for all creatures, Therein are fruit and palms having sheathed clusters, Husked grain and fragrant herbs. Then which of the favours of your Lord will you deny? He created man of clay like earthenware, And He created Jinn from a flame of smokeless fire. Then which of the favours of your Lord will you deny? Lord of the two Easts, and of the two Wests, Then which of the favours of your Lord will you deny? He has made the two seas flow; their sides meet but between them is a barrier which they cannot across.

55/1-20

His beams of mercy precede all creations and are within all afflictions and difficulties. The world of cause and effect and reasoning is but a small facet of His cosmos and the unique oneness of His Essence. Indeed, His mercy manifests in all creational diversity and apparent dispersion. The worlds unfold according to His knowledge and decrees. How can any intelligent being deny His numerous signs? Diversity is founded upon His unity. He is the Source and the Destiny of all creations. Every experience belongs to one of the two seas. Good or bad, health or illness, night or day, life or death, seen or unseen. The two seas, or realms, meet in the Adamic being but each within its boundaries and limits. Human beings are the inter-space between these different entities. Man is the microcosm, which can reproduce all evils or all virtues.

Allah has created out of generous love, and thus He is the one worthy of adoration, glorification and trusting submission. Creations are at many levels and spheres of consciousness. The mineral, vegetative and animal are all below and within the human paradigm.

Every creation follows its appropriate pattern and purpose, which is made easy and natural for it to follow and live by. Whoever goes against the primal blueprint will experience the agitation of fire here and hereafter.

Purifying our bodies' thoughts and hearts along with trust and striving for higher consciousness prepares us for an awakening to subtle levels of knowledge. True contentment comes about when His perfection, power and presence are witnessed.

10.

ٱلرَّحْمَٰنُ ۝ عَلَّمَ ٱلْقُرْآنَ ۝ خَلَقَ ٱلْإِنسَٰنَ ۝ عَلَّمَهُ ٱلْبَيَانَ ۝ ٱلشَّمْسُ وَٱلْقَمَرُ بِحُسْبَانٍ ۝ وَٱلنَّجْمُ وَٱلشَّجَرُ يَسْجُدَانِ ۝ وَٱلسَّمَآءَ رَفَعَهَا وَوَضَعَ ٱلْمِيزَانَ ۝ أَلَّا تَطْغَوْا۟ فِى ٱلْمِيزَانِ ۝ وَأَقِيمُوا۟ ٱلْوَزْنَ بِٱلْقِسْطِ وَلَا تُخْسِرُوا۟ ٱلْمِيزَانَ ۝ وَٱلْأَرْضَ وَضَعَهَا لِلْأَنَامِ ۝ فِيهَا فَٰكِهَةٌ وَٱلنَّخْلُ ذَاتُ ٱلْأَكْمَامِ ۝ وَٱلْحَبُّ ذُو ٱلْعَصْفِ وَٱلرَّيْحَانُ ۝ فَبِأَىِّ ءَالَآءِ رَبِّكُمَا تُكَذِّبَانِ ۝ خَلَقَ ٱلْإِنسَٰنَ مِن صَلْصَٰلٍ كَٱلْفَخَّارِ ۝ وَخَلَقَ ٱلْجَآنَّ مِن مَّارِجٍ مِّن نَّارٍ ۝ فَبِأَىِّ ءَالَآءِ رَبِّكُمَا تُكَذِّبَانِ ۝ رَبُّ ٱلْمَشْرِقَيْنِ وَرَبُّ ٱلْمَغْرِبَيْنِ ۝ فَبِأَىِّ ءَالَآءِ رَبِّكُمَا تُكَذِّبَانِ ۝ مَرَجَ ٱلْبَحْرَيْنِ يَلْتَقِيَانِ ۝ بَيْنَهُمَا بَرْزَخٌ لَّا يَبْغِيَانِ ۝

Glorify the name of your Lord the Most High, Who has created and then proportioned; And Who measured and then guided, And Who brings forth pastures, Then dries them up (so they are) earth coloured. We shall make you recite so that you do not forget, except what Allah wills. Surely, He knows what is manifest and what is hidden. We shall make your way easy and smooth. Therefore remind if reminding will benefit. He who has fear will be reminded, But the most unfortunate one will avoid it. He who will burn in the great fire wherein he will neither live nor die. Indeed, he who had purified himself is successful, as he remembers the name of his Lord and prays. But you prefer the life of the world, while the Hereafter is better and more lasting. Indeed, this is in the earlier scriptures, the scriptures of Abraham and Moses.

87/1-19

11.

وَالشَّمْسِ وَضُحَاهَا
وَالْقَمَرِ إِذَا تَلَاهَا
وَالنَّهَارِ إِذَا جَلَّاهَا
وَاللَّيْلِ إِذَا يَغْشَاهَا
وَالسَّمَاءِ وَمَا بَنَاهَا
وَالْأَرْضِ وَمَا طَحَاهَا
وَنَفْسٍ وَمَا سَوَّاهَا
فَأَلْهَمَهَا فُجُورَهَا وَتَقْوَاهَا
قَدْ أَفْلَحَ مَنْ زَكَّاهَا
وَقَدْ خَابَ مَنْ دَسَّاهَا
كَذَّبَتْ ثَمُودُ بِطَغْوَاهَا
إِذِ انْبَعَثَ أَشْقَاهَا
فَقَالَ لَهُمْ رَسُولُ اللَّهِ نَاقَةَ اللَّهِ وَسُقْيَاهَا
فَكَذَّبُوهُ فَعَقَرُوهَا فَدَمْدَمَ عَلَيْهِمْ رَبُّهُمْ بِذَنْبِهِمْ فَسَوَّاهَا
وَلَا يَخَافُ عُقْبَاهَا

By the sun and its brightness, And the moon as it follows it, And the day when it reveals, And the night when it conceals, And the heaven and He who built it, And the earth and He who spread it, And the self *(nafs)* and He who perfected it, Then inspired it to (understand) the ways of evil and the ways of cautious awareness *(taqwā)*. He is indeed successful who purifies it (the self), and indeed he who covers (its faults) fails. The Thamud denied the truth in their rebellious transgressions, when the most despicable of them rushed forth, and the messenger of Allah said: It is Allah's she-camel so let her drink! But they denied him, and they hamstrung her, so Allah crushed them for their sin and flattened them. And He does not fear the consequences.

91/1-15

Love of this world is only a sample and indicator of the love of the Creator. Therefore the intelligent being realizes that the love of a beautiful object is, in reality, love of beauty itself. Without this realization worldly love would be a barrier for spiritual progress instead of a stimulus towards it. The sun is followed by the moon and day by night. Then there is earth and heavens, the lower self and cognitive self, which reflect the Divine Light. Witnessing and knowledge of Him is the purpose of life, without which we cannot attain lasting contentment and happiness.

Like the individual self, nations and societies can awaken to the prophetic way or can cause chaos and destruction.

All experiences occur within the imaginal faculty of the self. All existential realities take on their self-reality according to the state of the self. The heart and cognitive faculties complement the senses so that the self interacts in this world while connected to its Divine source, which is the cause of all realities.

12.

مَّا خَلْقُكُمْ وَلَا بَعْثُكُمْ إِلَّا كَنَفْسٍ وَاحِدَةٍ إِنَّ اللَّهَ سَمِيعٌ بَصِيرٌ

Your creation and your raising (from the dead) are only as (the creation and the raising of) a single soul. Indeed, Allah is Hearer and Seer.

31/28

13.

إِنَّا خَلَقْنَا الْإِنسَانَ مِن نُّطْفَةٍ أَمْشَاجٍ نَّبْتَلِيهِ فَجَعَلْنَاهُ سَمِيعًا بَصِيرًا

Behold! We created man from a drop of fluid to test him, so we made him hearing and seeing.

76/2

14.

وَلَقَدْ عَهِدْنَا إِلَىٰ آدَمَ مِن قَبْلُ فَنَسِيَ وَلَمْ نَجِدْ لَهُ عَزْمًا

And indeed We made a covenant with Adam, but he forgot; and We found no firm resolve in him.

20/115

15.

وَإِذْ قُلْنَا لِلْمَلَائِكَةِ اسْجُدُوا لِآدَمَ فَسَجَدُوا إِلَّا إِبْلِيسَ أَبَىٰ وَاسْتَكْبَرَ وَكَانَ مِنَ الْكَافِرِينَ وَقُلْنَا يَا آدَمُ اسْكُنْ أَنْتَ وَزَوْجُكَ الْجَنَّةَ وَكُلَا مِنْهَا رَغَدًا حَيْثُ شِئْتُمَا وَلَا تَقْرَبَا هَٰذِهِ الشَّجَرَةَ فَتَكُونَا مِنَ الظَّالِمِينَ فَأَزَلَّهُمَا الشَّيْطَانُ عَنْهَا فَأَخْرَجَهُمَا مِمَّا كَانَا فِيهِ وَقُلْنَا اهْبِطُوا بَعْضُكُمْ لِبَعْضٍ عَدُوٌّ وَلَكُمْ فِي الْأَرْضِ مُسْتَقَرٌّ وَمَتَاعٌ إِلَىٰ حِينٍ فَتَلَقَّىٰ آدَمُ مِنْ رَبِّهِ كَلِمَاتٍ فَتَابَ عَلَيْهِ إِنَّهُ هُوَ التَّوَّابُ الرَّحِيمُ

And when We said to the angels: Prostrate yourselves before Adam, they all fell prostrate except Iblīs. He refused and was proud, so he became one of the disbelievers *(kafirūn)*. And We said: O Adam! Dwell in this Garden, you and your wife, and eat freely from it whenever you will, but do not approach this tree or you will become one of the unjust. But Shaytān made them depart from the state in which they were; and We said: Go down from here as enemies to each other; there shall be a resting place and provision for you on earth for a time. Then Adam received words (of revelation) from his Lord, and He turned towards him. Surely He is the Relenting and the most Merciful.

2/34-37

Adam was created in the Heavenly Garden by Allah's will and had no prior experience of evil or disobedience. He was innocent, pure and without self-consciousness.

Through Shaytān, Adam was exposed to distraction and disobedience and thus the pain of separation and self-concern. This veil of reason and self-interest hides the ever-present One cause behind and within existence.

All creation is caught in the web of His mercy and grace. Thus satanic whisperings can become stimuli for discrimination, vigilance, obedience and illumined worship.

Allah's mercy and forgiveness is greater than we can comprehend. Evil whispers can easily be overcome by reference to His voice of truth within.

Man's weakness can be the driving force to call upon His Power and desired Attributes. Turning away from the lower tendencies will show us the light within the heart.

16.

وَإِمَّا يَنزَغَنَّكَ مِنَ الشَّيْطَانِ نَزْغٌ فَاسْتَعِذْ بِاللَّهِ إِنَّهُ هُوَ السَّمِيعُ الْعَلِيمُ

And if a whisper from the shaytān reaches you, seek refuge in Allah. Indeed He is the Hearer, the Knower.

41/36

17.

الَّذِينَ آمَنُوا يُقَاتِلُونَ فِي سَبِيلِ اللَّهِ وَالَّذِينَ كَفَرُوا يُقَاتِلُونَ فِي سَبِيلِ الطَّاغُوتِ فَقَاتِلُوا أَوْلِيَاءَ الشَّيْطَانِ إِنَّ كَيْدَ الشَّيْطَانِ كَانَ ضَعِيفًا

Those who have faith (īmān) do battle for the cause of Allah; and those who are disbelievers (kāfir) do battle for the objects of their devotion. So fight the friends of Shaytān. Indeed, Shaytān is ever weak.

4/76

18.

الشَّيْطَانُ يَعِدُكُمُ الْفَقْرَ وَيَأْمُرُكُم بِالْفَحْشَاءِ وَاللَّهُ يَعِدُكُم مَّغْفِرَةً مِّنْهُ وَفَضْلًا وَاللَّهُ وَاسِعٌ عَلِيمٌ

The Shaytān promises you poverty and bids you to commit wrong and detestable acts. But Allah promises you forgiveness from himself and bounty. Allah is all Embracing, Knowing.

2/268

19.

وَيَسْأَلُونَكَ عَنِ ٱلرُّوحِ قُلِ ٱلرُّوحُ مِنْ أَمْرِ رَبِّى وَمَآ أُوتِيتُم مِّنَ ٱلْعِلْمِ إِلَّا قَلِيلًا

And they will ask you concerning the Spirit (Rūh). Say: the Spirit is by command of my Lord, and of knowledge you have been given but a little.

17/85

20.

وَخَلَقَ ٱلْجَآنَّ مِن مَّارِجٍ مِّن نَّارٍ

And the invisible entities (jinn) He created from a flame of smokeless fire.

55/15

21.

كَلَّآ إِنَّا خَلَقْنَٰهُم مِّمَّا يَعْلَمُونَ

Nay, certainly we created them from what they know.

70/39

22.

إِنَّا كُلَّ شَىْءٍ خَلَقْنَٰهُ بِقَدَرٍ

Indeed, We have created everything according to a measure

54/49

As for the human spirit (rūh), it is a heavenly reflection of His light. It is the primal energy source, which contains His pattern, design and the pen through which His decrees manifest.

The Adamic form and physical structure is composed of earth and water, while the jinn and Shaytāns are composed of fire and air. Shaytān considered his make-up superior to Adam. Through reasoning he disobeyed Allah's commands. His vanity was borne of ignorance.

For in earth and water can be found the qualities of tranquility, clemency, perseverance and growth; whereas in fire and air are the qualities of heedlessness, insignificance, haste and incineration.

Allah is the Sublimely Perfect and all creation seeks Him.

The human self will only be content when it submits to Him unconditionally.

To Him all creation returns and will experience joy or grief according to self-purification and illumination of the soul.

The narrow path of truth is surrounded by pitfalls and dangers. Thus, constant awareness, vigilance and perseverance are needed to arrive at His Presence.

23.

إِلَيْهِ مَرْجِعُكُمْ جَمِيعًا وَعْدَاللَّهِ حَقًّا إِنَّهُ يَبْدَأُ الْخَلْقَ ثُمَّ يُعِيدُهُ لِيَجْزِيَ الَّذِينَ آمَنُوا وَعَمِلُوا الصَّالِحَاتِ بِالْقِسْطِ وَالَّذِينَ كَفَرُوا لَهُمْ شَرَابٌ مِنْ حَمِيمٍ وَعَذَابٌ أَلِيمٌ بِمَا كَانُوا يَكْفُرُونَ

To Him is the return of you all. It is a promise of Allah in truth. Indeed, He began creation, and then He reproduces it, that He may reward those who have faith and have done righteous works with equity. As for those in denial of truth, they will have a boiling drink and painful punishment because of their denial.

10/4

24.

قُلْ أَعُوذُ بِرَبِّ الْفَلَقِ
مِن شَرِّ مَا خَلَقَ
وَمِن شَرِّ غَاسِقٍ إِذَا وَقَبَ
وَمِن شَرِّ النَّفَّاثَاتِ فِي الْعُقَدِ
وَمِن شَرِّ حَاسِدٍ إِذَا حَسَدَ

Say: I seek refuge in the Lord of Daybreak, from the evil of what He has created, from the evil of the darkness when it is intense, And from the evil of malignant witchcraft, And from the evil of the envier when he envies

113/1-

CHAPTER SEVEN

PROPHETS AND MESSENGERS

The prophet is a human being who is subjected to all natural human ways and characteristics whilst connected to a unique reference point and source of guidance. He is the ultimate model of conduct for evolving human beings in that he acts in the right way and at the right time and in a way that is understood and approved by all people of intellect, wisdom and insight.

Prophethood transmits information regarding divine truths and realities, which include knowledge of the Creator's Essence, His Attributes and His creational ways, boundaries and intentions. All prophets and messengers expressed knowledge of God. Some also conveyed messages relating to boundaries, appropriate conduct and natural laws. The prophets' conduct and actions are a model of perfect human qualities, of generosity, understanding, sacrifice, justice, gentleness, firmness, courage and other virtuous qualities befitting God's representative on earth. Their leadership and care for fellow humans encompassed the weak, the needy, the good and evil, and especially those serious in the quest of gnosis. The life of the prophetic being reflects what is the proper path to the knowledge of God and what is to be avoided and transcended. All prophets and messengers were endowed with miracles and other inexplicable qualities and knowledge appropriate to their time and mission. The miracles of the Prophet Muhammad were the Qur'an and his noble way of living amongst the least civilized of human tribes.

The way and life of the Prophet Muhammad, his conduct, practices and teachings are a living illustration of the Qur'an. The outer human difficulties and afflictions of the Prophet are understandable in the light of the revolutionary changes and new directions he brought to individuals and society. The prophetic sacrifices in fulfilling the divine mission become of negligible significance compared to the inner delights and divine intimacies. When the inner battle is won, the outer and physical struggles are only a small price to pay.

PROPHETS IN THE QUR'AN

ARABIC	ENGLISH	ARABIC	ENGLISH
Al-Yasa'	Elisha	Sulayman	Soloman
Ayyūb	Job	'Uzair	Ezra
Dāwūd	David	Ya'qūb	Jacob
Hārūn	Aaron	Yahyā	John
Ibrāhīm*	Abraham	Yūnus	Jonah
Idrīs	Enoch	Yūsuf	Joseph
Ilyās	Elias	Zakarīyah	Zachariya
'Īsā*	Jesus	Shu'ayb	Shuaib
Ishāq	Isaac	Salih	Salih
Ismā'īl	Ishmael	Hud	Hud
Lūt Lot	Isaac	Dhu'l	Kifl
Mūsa*	Moses	Hizqil	Ezekial
Nūh*	Noah	Adam	Adam

* The firmly resolved prophets (*Ūlū al-'azm*) whose influences were universal.

1.

$$كَانَ النَّاسُ أُمَّةً وَاحِدَةً فَبَعَثَ اللَّهُ النَّبِيِّينَ مُبَشِّرِينَ وَمُنذِرِينَ وَأَنزَلَ مَعَهُمُ الْكِتَابَ بِالْحَقِّ لِيَحْكُمَ بَيْنَ النَّاسِ فِيمَا اخْتَلَفُوا فِيهِ وَمَا اخْتَلَفَ فِيهِ إِلَّا الَّذِينَ أُوتُوهُ مِن بَعْدِ مَا جَاءَتْهُمُ الْبَيِّنَاتُ بَغْيًا بَيْنَهُمْ فَهَدَى اللَّهُ الَّذِينَ آمَنُوا لِمَا اخْتَلَفُوا فِيهِ مِنَ الْحَقِّ بِإِذْنِهِ وَاللَّهُ يَهْدِي مَن يَشَاءُ إِلَىٰ صِرَاطٍ مُّسْتَقِيمٍ$$

Mankind was one community, and Allah sent the Prophets to bring good news and give warnings. With them He sent down the Book with the truth that it might decide between mankind wherein they differed. Those to whom the Book was given differed concerning it, even after clear proofs had come to them, through envy of each other. Allah, by His permission guided those with faith to the truth of that which they differed. Allah guides who He wills to a Straight path.

2/213

Mankind's origin is from the Adamic blueprint and thus of one essence. We all desire everlasting happiness.

2.

$$إِنَّ اللَّهَ اصْطَفَىٰ آدَمَ وَنُوحًا وَآلَ إِبْرَاهِيمَ وَآلَ عِمْرَانَ عَلَى الْعَالَمِينَ$$

Certainly, Allah preferred Adam and Noah and the family of Abraham and the family of Imran above all other beings.

3/33

Messengers and prophets simply transmitted and lived the truth regarding our divine origin. They were the perfect role models, connecting the physical/material realities with the unseen world of lights, angels and other energies. They personified His Mercy to the children of Adam and Eve.

To know the Creator, we must submit and surrender to His will and ways. This voluntary and sincere submission is the door to insight, unveiling and awakening to wisdom and knowledge. Turning away from the lower tendencies is the key to entry into higher realms of our spirituality.

3.

وَمَن يَرْغَبُ عَن مِّلَّةِ إِبْرَاهِيمَ إِلَّا مَن سَفِهَ نَفْسَهُ وَلَقَدِ اصْطَفَيْنَاهُ فِي الدُّنْيَا وَإِنَّهُ فِي الْآخِرَةِ لَمِنَ الصَّالِحِينَ
إِذْ قَالَ لَهُ رَبُّهُ أَسْلِمْ قَالَ أَسْلَمْتُ لِرَبِّ الْعَالَمِينَ
وَوَصَّى بِهَا إِبْرَاهِيمُ بَنِيهِ وَيَعْقُوبُ يَا بَنِيَّ إِنَّ اللَّهَ اصْطَفَى لَكُمُ الدِّينَ فَلَا تَمُوتُنَّ إِلَّا وَأَنتُم مُّسْلِمُونَ
أَمْ كُنتُمْ شُهَدَاءَ إِذْ حَضَرَ يَعْقُوبَ الْمَوْتُ إِذْ قَالَ لِبَنِيهِ مَا تَعْبُدُونَ مِن بَعْدِي قَالُوا نَعْبُدُ إِلَهَكَ وَإِلَهَ آبَائِكَ إِبْرَاهِيمَ وَإِسْمَاعِيلَ وَإِسْحَاقَ إِلَهًا وَاحِدًا وَنَحْنُ لَهُ مُسْلِمُونَ

And whoever forsakes the religion of Abraham has dishonoured himself? Certainly We chose him in the world, and indeed in the Hereafter he is among the righteous. When his Lord said unto him: Indeed submit! He said I have submitted to the Lord of the Worlds. Abraham directed his sons to this, as did Jacob (saying): O my sons! Indeed Allah has chosen for you the religion (dīn); therefore, do not die except as Muslims. Did you not witness when death came upon Jacob, he said: What will you worship after me? They said: your God, the God of your fathers, Abraham, Ishmael and Isaac. He is One God, and to him we have surrendered.

2/130-133

All of the messengers related the truth according to the language and culture of their time and their people. They were the reliable travel guides along the path of gnosis.

4.

وَمَا أَرْسَلْنَا مِن رَّسُولٍ إِلَّا بِلِسَانِ قَوْمِهِ لِيُبَيِّنَ لَهُمْ فَيُضِلُّ اللَّهُ مَن يَشَاءُ وَيَهْدِي مَن يَشَاءُ وَهُوَ الْعَزِيزُ الْحَكِيمُ

We never sent a messenger except with the language of his people, that he might make (the message) clear for them. Then Allah misleads whom He wills and guides whom He wills. He is the Mighty, the Wise.

14/4

5.

$$\text{وَجَاهِدُوا فِي اللَّهِ حَقَّ جِهَادِهِ هُوَ اجْتَبَاكُمْ وَمَا جَعَلَ عَلَيْكُمْ فِي الدِّينِ مِنْ حَرَجٍ مِلَّةَ أَبِيكُمْ إِبْرَاهِيمَ هُوَ سَمَّاكُمُ الْمُسْلِمِينَ مِنْ قَبْلُ وَفِي هَذَا لِيَكُونَ الرَّسُولُ شَهِيدًا عَلَيْكُمْ وَتَكُونُوا شُهَدَاءَ عَلَى النَّاسِ فَأَقِيمُوا الصَّلَاةَ وَآتُوا الزَّكَاةَ وَاعْتَصِمُوا بِاللَّهِ هُوَ مَوْلَاكُمْ فَنِعْمَ الْمَوْلَى وَنِعْمَ النَّصِيرُ}$$

Strive (jihād) for Allah with the diligence due to Him. He has chosen you and has not caused difficulty for you in the religion (dīn), the faith of your father Abraham. He has named you Muslims of old and in this (Book), that the messenger maybe a witness against you, and that you may be witnesses against mankind. So establish prayer (salāt) and pay alms tax (zakāt), and hold fast to Allah. He is your Protector, blessed Patron and a blessed Helper!

22/78

To realize the truth of Allah's oneness, struggle, sacrifice and sincere effort at all times are necessary. By reducing our concern for physical and the material, and by increasing our yearning and awareness of higher consciousness and meanings, we will achieve spiritual growth and illumination.

6.

$$\text{يَا أَيُّهَا النَّبِيُّ جَاهِدِ الْكُفَّارَ وَالْمُنَافِقِينَ وَاغْلُظْ عَلَيْهِمْ وَمَأْوَاهُمْ جَهَنَّمُ وَبِئْسَ الْمَصِيرُ}$$

O Prophet! Strive against the disbelievers and the hypocrites. Be firm against them. Their ultimate abode is hell, the worst destination.

9/73

7.

$$\text{وَإِذْ يَرْفَعُ إِبْرَاهِيمُ الْقَوَاعِدَ مِنَ الْبَيْتِ وَإِسْمَاعِيلُ رَبَّنَا تَقَبَّلْ مِنَّا إِنَّكَ أَنْتَ السَّمِيعُ الْعَلِيمُ}$$

And when Abraham and Ishmael were raising the foundations of the house (Abraham prayed): Our Lord! Accept this from us. Indeed, You alone are the Hearer, the Knower.

2/127

There will always be human beings who are only concerned about this world and are veiled from the subtle energies and lights, which govern the physical realms. They are the non-believers who 'cover' the truth. Their ignorance easily misleads others as it appeals to the lower self in us, thereby causing corruption and decadence in society as well.

Both Mary and her son, the Prophet Jesus, were great signs from Allah for people to take heed. Miracles and unusual events occur so that people take notice of the real purpose and meaning of life, which is to know, love and worship the glorious Creator.

All prophets and messengers propagated Islam (*submission to Allah*) as appropriate in their own time. The original intent of all religions was to guide to the path of submission, faith and trust in the One, All-Merciful Creator. The path of Islam (*dīn*) is a reliable map for safe arrival at the Divine Presence.

8.

قَالَتْ رَبِّ أَنَّىٰ يَكُونُ لِي وَلَدٌ وَلَمْ يَمْسَسْنِي بَشَرٌ قَالَ كَذَٰلِكِ ٱللَّهُ يَخْلُقُ مَا يَشَاءُ إِذَا قَضَىٰ أَمْرًا فَإِنَّمَا يَقُولُ لَهُ كُن فَيَكُونُ

She (Maryam) said: My Lord! How can I have a child when no man has touched me? He said: Even so Allah creates what He wills. When He decides on a thing, He says only: Be! and it is.

3/47

9.

قَالَتْ أَنَّىٰ يَكُونُ لِي غُلَامٌ وَلَمْ يَمْسَسْنِي بَشَرٌ وَلَمْ أَكُ بَغِيًّا
قَالَ كَذَٰلِكِ قَالَ رَبُّكِ هُوَ عَلَيَّ هَيِّنٌ وَلِنَجْعَلَهُ آيَةً لِلنَّاسِ وَرَحْمَةً مِّنَّا وَكَانَ أَمْرًا مَّقْضِيًّا

She said: how can I have a son when no mortal has touched me. Nor have I been unchaste. He said: Even so. Your Lord says it is easy for Me; and We shall make him a sign to men, and a Mercy from Us. And it was a matter that was decreed.

19/20-21

10.

يَا يَحْيَىٰ خُذِ ٱلْكِتَابَ بِقُوَّةٍ وَآتَيْنَاهُ ٱلْحُكْمَ صَبِيًّا

O John! Take hold of the Book. And We granted him wisdom even as a youth.

19/12

11.

وَبِكُفْرِهِمْ وَقَوْلِهِمْ عَلَىٰ مَرْيَمَ بُهْتَانًا عَظِيمًا وَقَوْلِهِمْ إِنَّا قَتَلْنَا الْمَسِيحَ عِيسَى ابْنَ مَرْيَمَ رَسُولَ اللَّهِ وَمَا قَتَلُوهُ وَمَا صَلَبُوهُ وَلَـٰكِن شُبِّهَ لَهُمْ وَإِنَّ الَّذِينَ اخْتَلَفُوا فِيهِ لَفِي شَكٍّ مِّنْهُ مَا لَهُم بِهِ مِنْ عِلْمٍ إِلَّا اتِّبَاعَ الظَّنِّ وَمَا قَتَلُوهُ يَقِينًا

It was not the prophet Jesus that was killed but someone else like him.

And because of their denial *(kufr)* and their utterance of a grave, false charge against Mary. And because of their saying: We killed the Messiah Jesus, son of Mary, Allah's messenger. They did not kill him or crucify him, but it appeared so to them. Indeed those who disagree are in doubt thereof. They have no knowledge of it, only conjecture. Most certainly they did not kill him.

4/156-157

12.

قُولُوا آمَنَّا بِاللَّهِ وَمَا أُنزِلَ إِلَيْنَا وَمَا أُنزِلَ إِلَىٰ إِبْرَاهِيمَ وَإِسْمَاعِيلَ وَإِسْحَاقَ وَيَعْقُوبَ وَالْأَسْبَاطِ وَمَا أُوتِيَ مُوسَىٰ وَعِيسَىٰ وَمَا أُوتِيَ النَّبِيُّونَ مِن رَّبِّهِمْ لَا نُفَرِّقُ بَيْنَ أَحَدٍ مِّنْهُمْ وَنَحْنُ لَهُ مُسْلِمُونَ

All prophets and messengers were faithful in their duties and truly reflected the one truth. Thus there is no difference between them in their knowledge of the one Lord of the universe.

Say (O Muslims): We believe in Allah and that which is revealed to us, and that which was revealed to Abraham, Ishmael, Isaac, Jacob, and the tribes; and that which Moses and Jesus received; and that which the prophets revealed from their Lord. We do not differentiate between any of them, and to Him we have surrendered.

2/136

The flood of Noah was an outcome of perpetual human transgression. The more he preached the path of submission and virtue, the more his people deserted him. Then physical nature erupted reflecting the human chaos. The prophet Noah was inspired by Allah to build and board the ark, which provided salvation for him and his followers.

His mercy upon mankind manifests in truths and miracles revealed to His chosen messengers whose worldly circumstances were different from each other. For the sensitive seeker, every moment brings new miracles and thrills to the heart.

13.

وَنَادَىٰ نُوحٌ رَّبَّهُ فَقَالَ رَبِّ إِنَّ ابْنِي مِنْ أَهْلِي وَإِنَّ وَعْدَكَ الْحَقُّ وَأَنتَ أَحْكَمُ الْحَاكِمِينَ
قَالَ يَا نُوحُ إِنَّهُ لَيْسَ مِنْ أَهْلِكَ إِنَّهُ عَمَلٌ غَيْرُ صَالِحٍ فَلَا تَسْأَلْنِ مَا لَيْسَ لَكَ بِهِ عِلْمٌ إِنِّي أَعِظُكَ أَن تَكُونَ مِنَ الْجَاهِلِينَ

And Noah cried to his Lord and said: My Lord! Indeed my son is of my household! Certainly your promise is true, and you are the Most Just of Judges. He said: O Noah! He is not of your household; his conduct is not righteous. So ask Me not about something of which you have no knowledge. I admonish you lest you be among the ignorant.

11/45-46

14.

قِيلَ يَا نُوحُ اهْبِطْ بِسَلَامٍ مِّنَّا وَبَرَكَاتٍ عَلَيْكَ وَعَلَىٰ أُمَمٍ مِّمَّن مَّعَكَ وَأُمَمٌ سَنُمَتِّعُهُمْ ثُمَّ يَمَسُّهُم مِّنَّا عَذَابٌ أَلِيمٌ

It was said: O Noah! Go down (from the mountain) with peace from Us and blessings upon you and all the nations (that will come) from you. (There will be other) nations whom we shall give enjoyment for a while, and then a painful torment will come upon them from Us.

11/48

15.

وَرَبُّكَ أَعْلَمُ بِمَن فِي السَّمَاوَاتِ وَالْأَرْضِ وَلَقَدْ فَضَّلْنَا بَعْضَ النَّبِيِّينَ عَلَىٰ بَعْضٍ وَآتَيْنَا دَاوُودَ زَبُورًا

Your Lord knows best all who are in the heavens and the earth. And we honoured some of the Prophets above others. To David We gave the Psalms.

17/55

16.

إِنَّا أَوْحَيْنَا إِلَيْكَ كَمَا أَوْحَيْنَا إِلَىٰ نُوحٍ وَالنَّبِيِّينَ مِن بَعْدِهِ ۚ وَأَوْحَيْنَا إِلَىٰ إِبْرَاهِيمَ وَإِسْمَاعِيلَ وَإِسْحَاقَ وَيَعْقُوبَ وَالْأَسْبَاطِ وَعِيسَىٰ وَأَيُّوبَ وَيُونُسَ وَهَارُونَ وَسُلَيْمَانَ ۚ وَآتَيْنَا دَاوُودَ زَبُورًا

Behold! We have revealed to you as we revealed to Noah and the prophets after him; as We revealed to Abraham, Ishmael, Isaac, Jacob and the tribes; and Jesus, Job, Jonah, Aaron and Solomon. And We bestowed upon David the Psalms.

4/163

17.

مُّحَمَّدٌ رَّسُولُ اللَّهِ ۚ وَالَّذِينَ مَعَهُ أَشِدَّاءُ عَلَى الْكُفَّارِ رُحَمَاءُ بَيْنَهُمْ ۖ تَرَاهُمْ رُكَّعًا سُجَّدًا يَبْتَغُونَ فَضْلًا مِّنَ اللَّهِ وَرِضْوَانًا ۖ سِيمَاهُمْ فِي وُجُوهِهِم مِّنْ أَثَرِ السُّجُودِ ۚ ذَٰلِكَ مَثَلُهُمْ فِي التَّوْرَاةِ ۚ وَمَثَلُهُمْ فِي الْإِنجِيلِ كَزَرْعٍ أَخْرَجَ شَطْأَهُ فَآزَرَهُ فَاسْتَغْلَظَ فَاسْتَوَىٰ عَلَىٰ سُوقِهِ يُعْجِبُ الزُّرَّاعَ لِيَغِيظَ بِهِمُ الْكُفَّارَ ۗ وَعَدَ اللَّهُ الَّذِينَ آمَنُوا وَعَمِلُوا الصَّالِحَاتِ مِنْهُم مَّغْفِرَةً وَأَجْرًا عَظِيمًا

Muhammad is the Messenger of Allah. Those who are with him strongly oppose those who cover up reality, and they are merciful amongst themselves. You see them bowing and prostrating, seeking grace from Allah. Their mark is on their faces from the traces of prostration. This is their description in the Torah. Their likeness in the Gospel is like sown corn that sends forth its shoot then strengthens it so that it thickens and grows up straight on its stalk, delighting the sowers while enraging the unbelievers. Allah has promised those among them who have faith and perform good actions, forgiveness and immense reward.

48/29

The seal of all prophets and messengers is Muhammad (peace be upon him) who brought forth the distillation of all previous teachings and knowledge.

The Muhammadi message is the final universal gift of the clear path until the end of time. The path of Islam is a universal code applicable at all times and by all people everywhere. Every path must have boundaries and limits, which are constricting, but the goal is the infinite glorious Source who is eternally boundless.

> The Muhammadi message is a universal call to leave the darkness caused by the veils of misconception and deception of the outer world. The message reminds us to return to the Divine Source in preparation for the self's departure from the material world and the limitations of time and space. The good news is that we are essentially divinely patterned lights, called souls, veiled temporarily by the self.

18.

وَكَذَلِكَ جَعَلْنَا لِكُلِّ نَبِيٍّ عَدُوًّا شَيَاطِينَ الْإِنسِ وَالْجِنِّ يُوحِي بَعْضُهُمْ إِلَىٰ بَعْضٍ زُخْرُفَ الْقَوْلِ غُرُورًا ۚ وَلَوْ شَاءَ رَبُّكَ مَا فَعَلُوهُ ۖ فَذَرْهُمْ وَمَا يَفْتَرُونَ

For every prophet We have appointed an adversary - Shaytān from among humankind and the invisible entities - who inspires each other with delusion by means of beguiling speech. If your Lord had willed, they would not have done so, so leave them alone with their designs.

6/112

19.

وَلَوْ شَاءَ اللَّهُ مَا أَشْرَكُوا ۗ وَمَا جَعَلْنَاكَ عَلَيْهِمْ حَفِيظًا ۖ وَمَا أَنتَ عَلَيْهِم بِوَكِيلٍ

Had Allah willed, they would not have associated anything (with him). We have not appointed you as a keeper over them, nor are you responsible for them.

6/107

20.

يَا أَيُّهَا النَّبِيُّ إِنَّا أَرْسَلْنَاكَ شَاهِدًا وَمُبَشِّرًا وَنَذِيرًا وَدَاعِيًا إِلَى اللَّهِ بِإِذْنِهِ وَسِرَاجًا مُّنِيرًا

O Prophet! Indeed, We have sent you as a witness and a bringer of good tidings and a warner; And as one who calls to Allah by His permission; and as a radiant light.

33/45-46

21.

وَمَا أَرْسَلْنَاكَ إِلَّا كَافَّةً لِّلنَّاسِ بَشِيرًا وَنَذِيرًا وَلَٰكِنَّ أَكْثَرَ النَّاسِ لَا يَعْلَمُونَ

We have sent you (O Muhammad) to the entirety of mankind as one who brings good news and a warning, but most of mankind have no knowledge.

34/28

22.

$$\text{هُوَ الَّذِي يُنَزِّلُ عَلَىٰ عَبْدِهِ آيَاتٍ بَيِّنَاتٍ لِيُخْرِجَكُم مِّنَ الظُّلُمَاتِ إِلَى النُّورِ وَإِنَّ اللَّهَ بِكُمْ لَرَءُوفٌ رَّحِيمٌ}}$$

He it is Who sends down clear signs to his surrendered servants in order to bring you out from darkness into light. Allah is Most-Compassionate and Merciful to you.

57/9

The reward of enlightenment is constant access to the source of perfection and eternal joy, which transcends all worldly limitations.

23.

$$\text{وَمَا أَرْسَلْنَاكَ إِلَّا رَحْمَةً لِّلْعَالَمِينَ}$$

We have sent you only as a mercy to all existence.

21/107

24.

$$\text{وَمَا تَسْأَلُهُمْ عَلَيْهِ مِنْ أَجْرٍ إِنْ هُوَ إِلَّا ذِكْرٌ لِّلْعَالَمِينَ}$$

You do not ask of them for it any reward. It is only a reminder for all mankind.

12/104

All the prophets and messengers are subject to human and existential situations like everyone else. They are, however, constantly connected to Allah, Who reveals to them what He wills, and they are fully content with knowledge of His decrees. They are truly the perfect, accessible role models.

25.

$$\text{قُل لَّا أَمْلِكُ لِنَفْسِي نَفْعًا وَلَا ضَرًّا إِلَّا مَا شَاءَ اللَّهُ وَلَوْ كُنتُ أَعْلَمُ الْغَيْبَ لَاسْتَكْثَرْتُ مِنَ الْخَيْرِ وَمَا مَسَّنِيَ السُّوءُ إِنْ أَنَا إِلَّا نَذِيرٌ وَبَشِيرٌ لِّقَوْمٍ يُؤْمِنُونَ}$$

Say: I do not contain any benefit or harm for myself except as Allah wills. Had I knowledge of the unseen, I should have abundance of good fortune and adversity would not touch me. However, I am only a warner and a bearer of good tidings to people with faith.

7/188

By yielding to His decrees and the prophetic ways, we shall realize desirable destinies here and in the Hereafter.

Allah's blessings are showered upon the last chosen Prophet and his family (peace and blessings of Allah be upon them). His angels bestow bounties and mercy upon the prophetic caravan and its followers in this life and the next. Sincere seekers remember the prophetic ways and refer to his perfections as a reliable reference.

The inner and outer qualities of the Messenger are most desired and emulated by all sincere seekers. We are like moons that draw light from the prophetic sun and the unconditional love and respect of the prophet brings about knowledge of Allah's original love for all of His creation.

26.

إِنَّكَ لَا تَهْدِي مَنْ أَحْبَبْتَ وَلَٰكِنَّ ٱللَّهَ يَهْدِي مَن يَشَآءُ وَهُوَ أَعْلَمُ بِٱلْمُهْتَدِينَ

Indeed, you cannot guide those you love, but Allah guides whom He wills. He has the best knowledge of those who are guided.

28/56

27.

يَٰٓأَيُّهَا ٱلَّذِينَ ءَامَنُوا۟ ٱسْتَجِيبُوا۟ لِلَّهِ وَلِلرَّسُولِ إِذَا دَعَاكُمْ لِمَا يُحْيِيكُمْ وَٱعْلَمُوٓا۟ أَنَّ ٱللَّهَ يَحُولُ بَيْنَ ٱلْمَرْءِ وَقَلْبِهِۦ وَأَنَّهُۥٓ إِلَيْهِ تُحْشَرُونَ

O you who have faith, respond to Allah and His messenger when He calls you to what will bring you to life. And know that Allah intervenes between a man and his heart, and that to Him you will be gathered.

8/24

28.

ٱلنَّبِىُّ أَوْلَىٰ بِٱلْمُؤْمِنِينَ مِنْ أَنفُسِهِمْ وَأَزْوَٰجُهُۥٓ أُمَّهَٰتُهُمْ وَأُو۟لُوا۟ ٱلْأَرْحَامِ بَعْضُهُمْ أَوْلَىٰ بِبَعْضٍ فِى كِتَٰبِ ٱللَّهِ مِنَ ٱلْمُؤْمِنِينَ وَٱلْمُهَٰجِرِينَ إِلَّآ أَن تَفْعَلُوٓا۟ إِلَىٰٓ أَوْلِيَآئِكُم مَّعْرُوفًا كَانَ ذَٰلِكَ فِى ٱلْكِتَٰبِ مَسْطُورًا

The Prophet is closer to the believers than they are to themselves, and his wives are as their mothers. Blood relations have closer ties to one another in the Book of Allah than the believers and emigrants (who migrated from Mecca), but you should still act kindly towards your friends. This is written in the Book.

33/6

29.

وَقَرْنَ فِي بُيُوتِكُنَّ وَلَا تَبَرَّجْنَ تَبَرُّجَ الْجَاهِلِيَّةِ الْأُولَىٰ وَأَقِمْنَ الصَّلَاةَ وَآتِينَ الزَّكَاةَ وَأَطِعْنَ اللَّهَ وَرَسُولَهُ إِنَّمَا يُرِيدُ اللَّهُ لِيُذْهِبَ عَنكُمُ الرِّجْسَ أَهْلَ الْبَيْتِ وَيُطَهِّرَكُمْ تَطْهِيرًا

Stay in your houses, and do not display yourselves like in the times of ignorance; and establish prayer and pay the alms tax *(zakāt)* and obey Allah and His Messenger. Allah's wish is to remove all impurity from you, O people of the house, and to purify you with a thorough purification.

33/33

30.

إِنَّ اللَّهَ وَمَلَائِكَتَهُ يُصَلُّونَ عَلَى النَّبِيِّ ۚ يَا أَيُّهَا الَّذِينَ آمَنُوا صَلُّوا عَلَيْهِ وَسَلِّمُوا تَسْلِيمًا

Surely, Allah and His angels bless the Prophet. O you who have faith, ask for blessings upon him and salute him with a worthy salutation.

33/56

31.

سُبْحَانَ الَّذِي أَسْرَىٰ بِعَبْدِهِ لَيْلًا مِّنَ الْمَسْجِدِ الْحَرَامِ إِلَى الْمَسْجِدِ الْأَقْصَى الَّذِي بَارَكْنَا حَوْلَهُ لِنُرِيَهُ مِنْ آيَاتِنَا ۚ إِنَّهُ هُوَ السَّمِيعُ الْبَصِيرُ

Glory be to Him Who took his servant on a journey by night from the mosque in Mecca *(Masjid al-Harām)* to the mosque in Jerusalem *(Masjid Al-Aqsa)* whose surroundings we have blessed, that We might show him some of our signs. Indeed, He is the Hearer, the Seer.

17/1

The Prophet reflects the divine perfection; he is gentle at heart, firm regarding truth, constant in conduct, just and fully accountable to Allah. He is modest, courageous, wise, empowered by Allah, and can only act according to His Master's will. This selfless being is illumined and illuminating. He is truly the ideal role model for the believer.

All the angelic entities and other unseen heavenly agencies are subservient to the prophetic being.

The root of all distractions and deceptions is lack of knowledge of the One (tawhīd). All aspects of duality and multiplicity are challenges, which could lead to the one source and essence. Without tawhīd, life's experiences can only exhaust and confuse the seeker.

The believers are constant in awareness of the Divine Presence and thus experience the state of joy as in paradise. Their hearts overflow with illumined faith.

The serious seeker is driven by a single-pointed passion to know Allah; as such, he is a trustworthy, obedient follower of the Messenger of Allah and His representative on earth - the masters of transformation and enlightenment.

32.

لَقَدْ جَاءَكُمْ رَسُولٌ مِنْ أَنفُسِكُمْ عَزِيزٌ عَلَيْهِ مَا عَنِتُّمْ حَرِيصٌ عَلَيْكُم بِالْمُؤْمِنِينَ رَءُوفٌ رَحِيمٌ

Indeed, a messenger has come to you from amongst yourselves. Your distress is grievous to him; he is full of concern for you; he is gentle and merciful to the believers.

9/128

33.

فَبِمَا رَحْمَةٍ مِنَ اللَّهِ لِنتَ لَهُمْ وَلَوْ كُنتَ فَظًّا غَلِيظَ الْقَلْبِ لَانفَضُّوا مِنْ حَوْلِكَ فَاعْفُ عَنْهُمْ وَاسْتَغْفِرْ لَهُمْ وَشَاوِرْهُمْ فِي الْأَمْرِ فَإِذَا عَزَمْتَ فَتَوَكَّلْ عَلَى اللَّهِ إِنَّ اللَّهَ يُحِبُّ الْمُتَوَكِّلِينَ

It was by the mercy of Allah that you were gentle with them (O Muhammad) for if you had been rough and hardhearted they would have dispersed from around you. So pardon them, and ask for forgiveness for them, and consult with them on important matters. And when you have made a decision, then put your trust in Allah. Surely, Allah loves those who put their trust (in Him).

3/159

34.

مَا كَانَ لِلنَّبِيِّ وَالَّذِينَ آمَنُوا أَن يَسْتَغْفِرُوا لِلْمُشْرِكِينَ وَلَوْ كَانُوا أُولِي قُرْبَىٰ مِن بَعْدِ مَا تَبَيَّنَ لَهُمْ أَنَّهُمْ أَصْحَابُ الْجَحِيمِ

It is not for the Prophet and those who have faith to ask forgiveness for the idolaters, even if they are close relatives, after it has become clear to them that they are companions of the fire.

9/113

35.

لَا تَجِدُ قَوْمًا يُؤْمِنُونَ بِاللَّهِ وَالْيَوْمِ الْآخِرِ يُوَادُّونَ مَنْ حَادَّ اللَّهَ وَرَسُولَهُ وَلَوْ كَانُوا آبَاءَهُمْ أَوْ أَبْنَاءَهُمْ أَوْ إِخْوَانَهُمْ أَوْ عَشِيرَتَهُمْ أُولَٰئِكَ كَتَبَ فِي قُلُوبِهِمُ الْإِيمَانَ وَأَيَّدَهُم بِرُوحٍ مِّنْهُ وَيُدْخِلُهُمْ جَنَّاتٍ تَجْرِي مِن تَحْتِهَا الْأَنْهَارُ خَالِدِينَ فِيهَا رَضِيَ اللَّهُ عَنْهُمْ وَرَضُوا عَنْهُ أُولَٰئِكَ حِزْبُ اللَّهِ أَلَا إِنَّ حِزْبَ اللَّهِ هُمُ الْمُفْلِحُونَ

You will not find people who believe in Allah and the last day loving anyone who opposes Allah and his messenger, though they be their fathers, their sons, their brothers, or their tribe. Allah has inscribed faith inside their hearts and reinforced them with a spirit from Himself, and He will admit them into gardens with rivers flowing underneath, wherein they will remain forever. Allah is pleased with them and they are pleased with Him. They are the party of Allah. Truly, the party of Allah is successful.

58/22

Allah's people are those who strive towards transformation to higher consciousness by transcending the lower self and gaining awareness of the perfection of the spirit within.

36.

يَا أَيُّهَا النَّبِيُّ حَسْبُكَ اللَّهُ وَمَنِ اتَّبَعَكَ مِنَ الْمُؤْمِنِينَ

O Prophet! Allah is sufficient for you and for the believers who follow you.

8/64

By following the prophetic path we are restricted from distractions from the real goal.

37.

قُلْ إِن كُنتُمْ تُحِبُّونَ اللَّهَ فَاتَّبِعُونِي يُحْبِبْكُمُ اللَّهُ وَيَغْفِرْ لَكُمْ ذُنُوبَكُمْ وَاللَّهُ غَفُورٌ رَّحِيمٌ

If you love Allah then follow me; Allah will love you and cover your wrong actions. Allah is forgiving, Merciful.

3/31

38.

تِلْكَ حُدُودُ اللَّهِ وَمَن يُطِعِ اللَّهَ وَرَسُولَهُ يُدْخِلْهُ جَنَّاتٍ تَجْرِي مِن تَحْتِهَا الْأَنْهَارُ خَالِدِينَ فِيهَا وَذَٰلِكَ الْفَوْزُ الْعَظِيمُ

These are the limits (imposed by) Allah. As for those who obey Allah and his messenger, We will admit them into Gardens under which rivers flow wherein they will remain forever. This is the Great Victory.

4/13

If we deny our boundaries we will not gain access to the inner boundless domains.

CHAPTER EIGHT

THE RELIGION (*Dīn*)

The word *dīn* implies a debt upon oneself to save oneself from the veils of falsehood, uncertainty, doubt, ignorance and worldly turmoil. The path of submission (*Islam*) begins by realizing human shortcomings and inadequacies. It continues by acquiring knowledge of appropriate conduct and action in the search for a contentment that is not transient. The successful seeker will come to realize that all basic human desires and motivations lead to a guiding light that is constantly and reliably available and present.

The conduct of the enlightened Muslim will lead him to spontaneous self-awareness and accountability resulting in a just and healthy community. All of the Islamic practices and laws lead toward heightened awareness, reflection as to intentions and thus appropriate actions. If the Qur'an and way of the prophets are followed, both in outer form and inner meaning, then without doubt, transformation and awakening occur.

The purpose of all spiritual practices is to realize the Divine Presence in every situation and at all times. The Qur'an defines all religions as being based on faithful submission and commitment to the truth. Therefore, the original message of every prophetically inspired religion was the

Islamic message though each was given a different name at a different time for a different people. All prophets and messengers professed the same truth and reflected the need of their people appropriately.

The fountain of Islam is transformative worship (*'ibādah*) and appropriate conduct towards oneself, creation and the Creator. The final message of Islam as relayed by the prophet Muhammad (peace be upon him) contains all that is needed for spiritual health and enlightenment for all people, times and societies.

The practices and rituals of Islam contain great disciplines for breaking normative behaviour and unhealthy habits. The limitations and restrictions of these practices and rituals are extremely beneficial as they facilitate the development of spiritual knowledge, which only becomes known after the fact. As an example, the outer difficulties of fasting provide a great deal of awareness and sensitivity that illumines the heart and opens up subtle wisdom, guidance, compassion, patience and tolerance. All difficulties and hardships result in immense progress and openings for the believers and followers of the path. The ultimate abode is in the security and in the presence of the One Lord of all creations.

a. Living Islam, faith (*imān*), excellence (*ihsān*)

1.

إِنَّ الدِّينَ عِندَ اللَّهِ الْإِسْلَامُ ۗ وَمَا اخْتَلَفَ الَّذِينَ أُوتُوا الْكِتَابَ إِلَّا مِن بَعْدِ مَا جَاءَهُمُ الْعِلْمُ بَغْيًا بَيْنَهُمْ ۗ وَمَن يَكْفُرْ بِآيَاتِ اللَّهِ فَإِنَّ اللَّهَ سَرِيعُ الْحِسَابِ

Truly, the religion with Allah is Islam. Those who received the Book differed through mutual envy only after knowledge came to them. Whoever disbelieves the revelations of Allah then surely Allah is Swift in Reckoning.
3/19

The path of enlightenment is based on submission to truth at all transient levels of reality whilst being committed to what is prescribed in the Qur'an and the way of the prophet towards realization of the eternal truth of the One.

2.

فَمَن يُرِدِ اللَّهُ أَن يَهْدِيَهُ يَشْرَحْ صَدْرَهُ لِلْإِسْلَامِ ۖ وَمَن يُرِدْ أَن يُضِلَّهُ يَجْعَلْ صَدْرَهُ ضَيِّقًا حَرَجًا كَأَنَّمَا يَصَّعَّدُ فِي السَّمَاءِ ۚ كَذَٰلِكَ يَجْعَلُ اللَّهُ الرِّجْسَ عَلَى الَّذِينَ لَا يُؤْمِنُونَ

Whomsoever Allah wishes to guide, He opens his heart to Islam, and whomever He wishes to send astray, He causes his heart to become closed and narrow as if he were engaged in a sheer ascent. Thus Allah places His wrath upon those who do not believe.
6/125

With submission comes deeper understanding of the human make-up, the hierarchy of needs, and the foundation of creation with its primal yearning and adoration of Allah's perfections. Everything in existence glorifies Him.

3.

وَمَن كَفَرَ فَلَا يَحْزُنكَ كُفْرُهُ ۚ إِلَيْنَا مَرْجِعُهُمْ فَنُنَبِّئُهُم بِمَا عَمِلُوا ۚ إِنَّ اللَّهَ عَلِيمٌ بِذَاتِ الصُّدُورِ نُمَتِّعُهُمْ قَلِيلًا ثُمَّ نَضْطَرُّهُمْ إِلَىٰ عَذَابٍ غَلِيظٍ

Whoever denies let not his disbelief sadden you. They will return to Us and We shall inform them about their actions. Allah knows the true condition of the hearts. We will let them enjoy themselves a little, then drive them to a harsh punishment.
31/23-24

Those who deny the path of enlightenment are in constant affliction, doubt and failure. All this leads to the ultimate fire of darkness and loss.

The ultimate fruit of spiritual development is awareness and witnessing of the One, and total reliance on His guidance.

4.

وَمَنْ أَحْسَنُ دِينًا مِمَّنْ أَسْلَمَ وَجْهَهُ لِلَّهِ وَهُوَ مُحْسِنٌ وَاتَّبَعَ مِلَّةَ إِبْرَاهِيمَ حَنِيفًا وَاتَّخَذَ اللَّهُ إِبْرَاهِيمَ خَلِيلًا

Who could have a better religion *(dīn)* than one who submits himself completely to Allah while doing good and following the tradition of Abraham the upright? Allah chose Abraham as an intimate friend.

4/125

5.

وَأَنْ أَقِمْ وَجْهَكَ لِلدِّينِ حَنِيفًا وَلَا تَكُونَنَّ مِنَ الْمُشْرِكِينَ

And turn your face towards the path of pure, natural faith and never be amongst those who associate with Allah.

10/105

Knowledge of God is based on knowledge of His Qualities, Attributes and the all-pervading Divine Essence.

6.

أَفَغَيْرَ دِينِ اللَّهِ يَبْغُونَ وَلَهُ أَسْلَمَ مَنْ فِي السَّمَاوَاتِ وَالْأَرْضِ طَوْعًا وَكَرْهًا وَإِلَيْهِ يُرْجَعُونَ

Is it other than the way of Allah that you seek, when everything in the heavens and earth submits to Him either willingly or unwillingly? To Him they will be returned.

3/83

All prophetically revealed books have emanated from the same Divine Source and call for submission and obedience to His will and purpose and thus free from the whisperings of the ego.

7.

صِبْغَةَ اللَّهِ وَمَنْ أَحْسَنُ مِنَ اللَّهِ صِبْغَةً وَنَحْنُ لَهُ عَابِدُونَ

The colouring is Allah's. Who is better than Allah at colouring? We are His worshippers.

2/138

8.

وَلَا تُجَادِلُوا أَهْلَ الْكِتَابِ إِلَّا بِالَّتِي هِيَ أَحْسَنُ إِلَّا الَّذِينَ ظَلَمُوا مِنْهُمْ وَقُولُوا آمَنَّا بِالَّذِي أُنزِلَ إِلَيْنَا وَأُنزِلَ إِلَيْكُمْ وَإِلَٰهُنَا وَإِلَٰهُكُمْ وَاحِدٌ وَنَحْنُ لَهُ مُسْلِمُونَ

Do not argue with the People of the Book unless it is in the kindest way, except with those among them who do wrong. Say: We believe in that which has been revealed to us and revealed to you. Our God and your God is One, and we submit to Him.

29/46

It is appropriate to discuss revealed knowledge about the one God with other people of 'divine books' with gentleness and compassion.

9.

يَا أَيُّهَا الَّذِينَ آمَنُوا ارْكَعُوا وَاسْجُدُوا وَاعْبُدُوا رَبَّكُمْ وَافْعَلُوا الْخَيْرَ لَعَلَّكُمْ تُفْلِحُونَ ۩ وَجَاهِدُوا فِي اللَّهِ حَقَّ جِهَادِهِ هُوَ اجْتَبَاكُمْ وَمَا جَعَلَ عَلَيْكُمْ فِي الدِّينِ مِنْ حَرَجٍ مِلَّةَ أَبِيكُمْ إِبْرَاهِيمَ هُوَ سَمَّاكُمُ الْمُسْلِمِينَ مِن قَبْلُ وَفِي هَٰذَا لِيَكُونَ الرَّسُولُ شَهِيدًا عَلَيْكُمْ وَتَكُونُوا شُهَدَاءَ عَلَى النَّاسِ فَأَقِيمُوا الصَّلَاةَ وَآتُوا الزَّكَاةَ وَاعْتَصِمُوا بِاللَّهِ هُوَ مَوْلَاكُمْ فَنِعْمَ الْمَوْلَىٰ وَنِعْمَ النَّصِيرُ

O you who have faith, bow down, prostrate yourselves, worship your Lord, and do good so that hopefully you may prosper. Strive for Allah with the endeavour that is due to Him. He has chosen you and not placed any hardships upon you in the religion. It is the faith of your father Abraham. He has named you Muslims before and now so that the messenger maybe a witnesser upon you and that you may be witnesses against mankind. So establish prayer, pay the alms tax and hold fast to Allah. He is your Protector, the best Protector - and a blessed Helper.

22/77-78

The inner and outer efforts toward perfection will continue for all believers who strive for His knowledge. Outer worship and obedience to the prophetic way must be matched by the inner quality of purposeful intention and purity of heart.

Knowledge of Allah is the ultimate reward. This gnosis is the source of eternal joy in this life and the Hereafter. Without the light of enlightenment, we simply flounder in self-perpetuated darkness and doubt.

Those who journey with light are indeed much different from who blunder through haphazardly.

10.

أَوَمَن كَانَ مَيْتًا فَأَحْيَيْنَاهُ وَجَعَلْنَا لَهُ نُورًا يَمْشِي بِهِ فِي النَّاسِ كَمَن مَّثَلُهُ فِي الظُّلُمَاتِ لَيْسَ بِخَارِجٍ مِّنْهَا كَذَٰلِكَ زُيِّنَ لِلْكَافِرِينَ مَا كَانُوا يَعْمَلُونَ

Is one who was dead and whom We brought to life, providing him with a light by which to walk among people, the same as someone who is in utter darkness, unable to emerge from it? The actions of those who disbelieve seem attractive to them.

6/122

In the world of causality, every action will have its appropriate result and effect but not always as expected. Our duty is to be sincere, obey His commands and make a constant effort towards inner freedom and illumined reliance upon Allah.

11.

آمَنَ الرَّسُولُ بِمَا أُنزِلَ إِلَيْهِ مِن رَّبِّهِ وَالْمُؤْمِنُونَ كُلٌّ آمَنَ بِاللَّهِ وَمَلَائِكَتِهِ وَكُتُبِهِ وَرُسُلِهِ لَا نُفَرِّقُ بَيْنَ أَحَدٍ مِّن رُّسُلِهِ وَقَالُوا سَمِعْنَا وَأَطَعْنَا غُفْرَانَكَ رَبَّنَا وَإِلَيْكَ الْمَصِيرُ لَا يُكَلِّفُ اللَّهُ نَفْسًا إِلَّا وُسْعَهَا لَهَا مَا كَسَبَتْ وَعَلَيْهَا مَا اكْتَسَبَتْ رَبَّنَا لَا تُؤَاخِذْنَا إِن نَّسِينَا أَوْ أَخْطَأْنَا رَبَّنَا وَلَا تَحْمِلْ عَلَيْنَا إِصْرًا كَمَا حَمَلْتَهُ عَلَى الَّذِينَ مِن قَبْلِنَا رَبَّنَا وَلَا تُحَمِّلْنَا مَا لَا طَاقَةَ لَنَا بِهِ وَاعْفُ عَنَّا وَاغْفِرْ لَنَا وَارْحَمْنَا أَنتَ مَوْلَانَا فَانصُرْنَا عَلَى الْقَوْمِ الْكَافِرِينَ

Spontaneous awareness, focused intention and appropriate action are the foundations of a successful life. Ultimately, real success belongs to Him and those who have abandoned unto Him.

The messenger believes in what has been revealed to him from his Lord and so do the believers. Each one has faith in Allah and believes in His angels and the Books and His messengers. We make no distinction between any of His messengers. They say: We hear and we obey – forgive us our Lord! You are our journey's end. Allah does not impose on any person except to his capacity. He obtains the reward for that which he has earned, and he is responsible for that which he has earned. O Lord, do not charge us if we forget or make a mistake! O Lord do not place on us burdens like the burdens placed on those before us! O Lord do not allow us to carry that which we have not the strength to bear! Pardon us, forgive us and have mercy on us. You are our Master, so grant us victory over those who disbelieve.

2/285-286

12.

الَّذِينَ إِن مَّكَّنَّاهُمْ فِي الْأَرْضِ أَقَامُوا الصَّلَاةَ وَآتَوُا الزَّكَاةَ وَأَمَرُوا بِالْمَعْرُوفِ وَنَهَوْا عَنِ الْمُنكَرِ وَلِلَّهِ عَاقِبَةُ الْأُمُورِ

Those, who if We give them power in the land, establish prayer, pay the alms tax, command what is right and forbid what is wrong. The end result of all matters is with Allah.

22/41

13.

فَإِذَا قَضَيْتُمُ الصَّلَاةَ فَاذْكُرُوا اللَّهَ قِيَامًا وَقُعُودًا وَعَلَىٰ جُنُوبِكُمْ ۚ فَإِذَا اطْمَأْنَنتُمْ فَأَقِيمُوا الصَّلَاةَ ۚ إِنَّ الصَّلَاةَ كَانَتْ عَلَى الْمُؤْمِنِينَ كِتَابًا مَّوْقُوتًا

When you have finished prayer, remember Allah standing, sitting and lying down. When you are established in safety (not fearing attack) keep up the (normal) prayer. The prayer is enjoined on the believers at prescribed times.

4/103

14.

الَّذِينَ هُمْ عَلَىٰ صَلَاتِهِمْ دَائِمُونَ وَالَّذِينَ فِي أَمْوَالِهِمْ حَقٌّ مَّعْلُومٌ لِّلسَّائِلِ وَالْمَحْرُومِ

Those who are perpetually engaged in worship, And in whose wealth there is an acknowledged right, for the beggar and the destitute.

70/23-25

15.

الَّذِينَ يَسْتَمِعُونَ الْقَوْلَ فَيَتَّبِعُونَ أَحْسَنَهُ ۚ أُولَٰئِكَ الَّذِينَ هَدَاهُمُ اللَّهُ ۖ وَأُولَٰئِكَ هُمْ أُولُو الْأَلْبَابِ

Those who listen to the word and follow the best of it, they are the ones who Allah has guided. They posses deep understanding.

39/18

Prayer is at many levels, ranging from the formal performance to the state of constant remembrance. It begins by submission, or offering, and its end is realizing Allah's bounties and care for creation according to the limits of their potential.

Ignorance, misconception and hypocrisy are the dark veils, which cover those who are not in sincere surrender to Him.

Without a pure heart, the human being is inwardly like a dead corpse with an animated physiology. It is by means of a wholesome heart that the faculty of cognition is developed leading to enlightenment.

Performance of outer obligations and acceptance of boundaries are essential steps towards witnessing His boundless Light and delight through the purified soul.

16.

فَوَيْلٌ لِّلْمُصَلِّينَ
الَّذِينَ هُمْ عَن صَلَاتِهِمْ سَاهُونَ

Woe to those who pray and are inattentive during their prayer.

107/4-5

17.

فَإِنَّكَ لَا تُسْمِعُ الْمَوْتَىٰ وَلَا تُسْمِعُ الصُّمَّ الدُّعَاءَ إِذَا وَلَّوْا مُدْبِرِينَ
وَمَا أَنتَ بِهَادِ الْعُمْيِ عَن ضَلَالَتِهِمْ ۖ إِن تُسْمِعُ إِلَّا مَن يُؤْمِنُ بِآيَاتِنَا فَهُم مُّسْلِمُونَ

Indeed, you cannot make the dead hear, nor can you make those who are deaf to the call hear when they turn their backs in flight. And you cannot guide the blind from their misguidance. You will only make those hear who have faith in Our signs so they shall submit.

30/52-53

The path of Islam is founded upon love and trust in Allah and thus acceptance of His decrees, along with realization of the perfection of the moment. From this wise and just position, struggle, sacrifice and striving will only bring about greater success and witnessing of His effulgent Presence.

18.

يَا أَيُّهَا الَّذِينَ آمَنُوا مَن يَرْتَدَّ مِنكُمْ عَن دِينِهِ فَسَوْفَ يَأْتِي اللَّهُ بِقَوْمٍ يُحِبُّهُمْ وَيُحِبُّونَهُ أَذِلَّةٍ عَلَى الْمُؤْمِنِينَ أَعِزَّةٍ عَلَى الْكَافِرِينَ يُجَاهِدُونَ فِي سَبِيلِ اللَّهِ وَلَا يَخَافُونَ لَوْمَةَ لَائِمٍ ۚ ذَٰلِكَ فَضْلُ اللَّهِ يُؤْتِيهِ مَن يَشَاءُ ۚ وَاللَّهُ وَاسِعٌ عَلِيمٌ

O you who believe, If any of you turn away from Allah's way, He will bring forth a people whom He loves and who love Him, humble to the believers, vigorous and strong against whatever contravenes belief, who strive in the way of Allah and so do not fear any blame. Such is the grace of Allah that He gives to whomever He wills. Allah is Boundless, All-Knowing.

5/54

19.

وَمِنْهُمْ أُمِّيُّونَ لَا يَعْلَمُونَ الْكِتَابَ إِلَّا أَمَانِيَّ وَإِنْ هُمْ إِلَّا يَظُنُّونَ

Some of them are illiterate, knowing nothing of the Book but wishful thinking; they only speculate.

2/78

20.

يَا أَيُّهَا الَّذِينَ آمَنُوا كُتِبَ عَلَيْكُمُ الصِّيَامُ كَمَا كُتِبَ عَلَى الَّذِينَ مِنْ قَبْلِكُمْ لَعَلَّكُمْ تَتَّقُونَ

O You who have faith. Fasting is prescribed for you, as it was prescribed to those before you, so that hopefully you will have cautious awareness.

2/183

21.

شَهْرُ رَمَضَانَ الَّذِي أُنْزِلَ فِيهِ الْقُرْآنُ هُدًى لِلنَّاسِ وَبَيِّنَاتٍ مِنَ الْهُدَى وَالْفُرْقَانِ فَمَنْ شَهِدَ مِنْكُمُ الشَّهْرَ فَلْيَصُمْهُ وَمَنْ كَانَ مَرِيضًا أَوْ عَلَى سَفَرٍ فَعِدَّةٌ مِنْ أَيَّامٍ أُخَرَ يُرِيدُ اللَّهُ بِكُمُ الْيُسْرَ وَلَا يُرِيدُ بِكُمُ الْعُسْرَ وَلِتُكْمِلُوا الْعِدَّةَ وَلِتُكَبِّرُوا اللَّهَ عَلَى مَا هَدَاكُمْ وَلَعَلَّكُمْ تَشْكُرُونَ

The month of Ramadān is the one in which the Qur'an was sent down as a guidance for mankind with clear signs containing guidance and discrimination. Any of you who are present in the month should fast it, but any of you who are ill or on a journey should fast a number of other days. Allah desires ease for you. He does not desire difficulty for you. You should complete the number of days and proclaim Allah's greatness for the guidance He has given you, so that hopefully you may be thankful.

2/185

Every experience, existence and meaning of a subtle, original pattern and the one source. The great prophet Abraham built the symbolic house of God as a paradigm for the ever-present spiritual sanctuary towards which the seekers turn.

Restriction and constriction in fasting and other acts of abstinence are necessary gates to subtle knowledge and insights. The spiritual openings and lights are already there but we are distracted from them by the lower self, its tendencies, demands and veils. Therefore, abstention and restrictions of worldly interactions are necessary steps towards the real ever lasting truth.

Formal pilgrimage to His House is both a personal and social step towards realizing Allah's presence both in this world and beyond. All worship is acts of yearning and dedication to the One Lord.

It is also natural for societies or communities to have amongst them people whose spiritual awareness and knowledge is higher than the average. These evolved beings are good example for virtuous and goodly life.

22.

إِنَّ أَوَّلَ بَيْتٍ وُضِعَ لِلنَّاسِ لَلَّذِى بِبَكَّةَ مُبَارَكاً وَهُدًى لِّلْعَالَمِينَ ۝ فِيهِ ءَايَـٰتٌۢ بَيِّنَـٰتٌ مَّقَامُ إِبْرَاهِيمَ وَمَن دَخَلَهُۥ كَانَ ءَامِناً وَلِلَّهِ عَلَى ٱلنَّاسِ حِجُّ ٱلْبَيْتِ مَنِ ٱسْتَطَاعَ إِلَيْهِ سَبِيلاً وَمَن كَفَرَ فَإِنَّ ٱللَّهَ غَنِىٌّ عَنِ ٱلْعَالَمِينَ ۝

Indeed, The first sanctuary appointed for people was that in Bakkah (*Mecca*), a blessed place, wherein is guidance for mankind. In it are clear signs, the place where Abraham stood up to pray. Whoever enters it is safe...

3/96-97

23.

ٱلْحَجُّ أَشْهُرٌ مَّعْلُومَـٰتٌ فَمَن فَرَضَ فِيهِنَّ ٱلْحَجَّ فَلَا رَفَثَ وَلَا فُسُوقَ وَلَا جِدَالَ فِى ٱلْحَجِّ وَمَا تَفْعَلُوا۟ مِنْ خَيْرٍ يَعْلَمْهُ ٱللَّهُ وَتَزَوَّدُوا۟ فَإِنَّ خَيْرَ ٱلزَّادِ ٱلتَّقْوَىٰ وَٱتَّقُونِ يَـٰٓأُو۟لِى ٱلْأَلْبَـٰبِ

The pilgrimage takes place during certain well-known months. Whoever undertakes the obligation of the pilgrimage must refrain from sexual relations, wrongdoing and any quarreling during pilgrimage. Whatever good you do Allah knows it. Take provisions, but the best provision is awareness of Allah. So be cautiously aware of Me, O people who posses inner understanding.

2/197

24.

وَلْتَكُن مِّنكُمْ أُمَّةٌ يَدْعُونَ إِلَى ٱلْخَيْرِ وَيَأْمُرُونَ بِٱلْمَعْرُوفِ وَيَنْهَوْنَ عَنِ ٱلْمُنكَرِ وَأُو۟لَـٰٓئِكَ هُمُ ٱلْمُفْلِحُونَ

And let there be a party from among you who invite to what is best, enjoin right conduct and prohibit wrong. They are the successful ones.

3/104

b. Correct Transactions

1.

إِنَّ الَّذِينَ آمَنُوا وَهَاجَرُوا وَجَاهَدُوا بِأَمْوَالِهِمْ وَأَنفُسِهِمْ فِي سَبِيلِ اللَّهِ وَالَّذِينَ آوَوا وَّنَصَرُوا أُولَٰئِكَ بَعْضُهُمْ أَوْلِيَاءُ بَعْضٍ ۚ وَالَّذِينَ آمَنُوا وَلَمْ يُهَاجِرُوا إِمَا لَكُم مِّن وَلَايَتِهِم مِّن شَيْءٍ حَتَّىٰ يُهَاجِرُوا ۚ وَإِنِ اسْتَنصَرُوكُمْ فِي الدِّينِ فَعَلَيْكُمُ النَّصْرُ إِلَّا عَلَىٰ قَوْمٍ بَيْنَكُمْ وَبَيْنَهُم مِّيثَاقٌ ۗ وَاللَّهُ بِمَا تَعْمَلُونَ بَصِيرٌ

Indeed those who have faith and have emigrated, who have striven in the way of Allah with their wealth and themselves, and those who have given refuge and help; they are the friends and protectors of one another. And as for those who believe but do not emigrate, they are not in any way responsible for their protection until they emigrate. But if they seek help in respect of Allah's way, it is your duty to help them, except against people with whom you have a treaty with. And Allah sees what you do.

8/72

The reward of all struggles and sacrifice is outer success accompanied by inner access to Him. Real success relates to sustainable inner happiness and contentment, and that depends on the extent of one's belief and knowledge of Allah and action in His way. This illumined path will bring inner contentment, calm and sustained joy.

2.

وَيَا قَوْمِ أَوْفُوا الْمِكْيَالَ وَالْمِيزَانَ بِالْقِسْطِ ۖ وَلَا تَبْخَسُوا النَّاسَ أَشْيَاءَهُمْ وَلَا تَعْثَوْا فِي الْأَرْضِ مُفْسِدِينَ

O My people, fulfill the measure and weight with justice. Do not diminish the value of peoples' goods and do not act in a wicked, corrupt manner.

11/85

The seeker needs courage, trust, and cautious awareness of the Almighty Lord.
Real piety relates to fairness, justice and generous deeds and love for others in His creation.

Constant grooming of the self, awareness of the lower tendencies, responsibility and accountability are essential for spiritual growth. Selfish acts, greed, covetousness and other evil habits, will block or divert enlightenment and freedom with illusions of the independent self or reliance upon one's ego.

Prohibitions and restricted freedom in actions are necessary for mankind to keep within the natural boundaries. Allah's path is the safe highway code to be followed and strictly adhered to for salvation and awakening to the spirit within and joyfulness in all circumstances.

3.

لَن تَنَالُوا ٱلۡبِرَّ حَتَّىٰ تُنفِقُوا مِمَّا تُحِبُّونَۚ وَمَا تُنفِقُوا مِن شَيۡءٖ فَإِنَّ ٱللَّهَ بِهِۦ عَلِيمٌ

You will not attain piety until you spend from what you love. Whatever you give away, Allah knows it.

3/92

4.

وَمَنۡ أَحۡسَنُ قَوۡلٗا مِّمَّن دَعَآ إِلَى ٱللَّهِ وَعَمِلَ صَٰلِحٗا وَقَالَ إِنَّنِي مِنَ ٱلۡمُسۡلِمِينَ

Who is better in speech than one who summons to Allah, acts correctly and says: I am of those who surrender.

41/33

5.

وَلَكُمۡ فِي ٱلۡقِصَاصِ حَيَوٰةٞ يَٰٓأُوْلِي ٱلۡأَلۡبَٰبِ لَعَلَّكُمۡ تَتَّقُونَ

And there is life for you in requital, O people of understanding, that hopefully you will be cautiously aware.

2/179

6.

يَٰٓأَيُّهَا ٱلَّذِينَ ءَامَنُوٓا۟ إِنَّمَا ٱلۡخَمۡرُ وَٱلۡمَيۡسِرُ وَٱلۡأَنصَابُ وَٱلۡأَزۡلَٰمُ رِجۡسٞ مِّنۡ عَمَلِ ٱلشَّيۡطَٰنِ فَٱجۡتَنِبُوهُ لَعَلَّكُمۡ تُفۡلِحُونَ

O you who have faith intoxicants, gambling, idols and divining arrows are impure actions of *Shaytān*. Avoid them completely so that you may be successful.

5/90

7.

اَلَّذِينَ يَأْكُلُونَ الرِّبَا لَا يَقُومُونَ إِلَّا كَمَا يَقُومُ الَّذِي يَتَخَبَّطُهُ الشَّيْطَانُ مِنَ الْمَسِّ ذَلِكَ بِأَنَّهُمْ قَالُوا إِنَّمَا الْبَيْعُ مِثْلُ الرِّبَا وَأَحَلَّ اللَّهُ الْبَيْعَ وَحَرَّمَ الرِّبَا فَمَنْ جَاءَهُ مَوْعِظَةٌ مِنْ رَبِّهِ فَانْتَهَى فَلَهُ مَا سَلَفَ وَأَمْرُهُ إِلَى اللَّهِ وَمَنْ عَادَ فَأُولَئِكَ أَصْحَابُ النَّارِ هُمْ فِيهَا خَالِدُونَ

Those who practice usury will not rise, except as one struck down by the devil's touch. That is because they say: Trade is the same as usury. But Allah has permitted trade, and He has forbidden usury. Whoever is given a warning by his Lord and then desists, can keep what he received in the past and his affair is Allah's concern. But all who return to it (usury) will be the Companions of hell (*jahannam*). Therein they will abide.

2/275

Usury and other unhealthy habits of selfishness and greed can only lead to greater injustices and disturbances.

Virtuous and moral conduct is essential for the inner health of the seeker of truth. Knowledge of Qur'an and the teachings of the Messenger are essential for safe passage. Outer limitations and laws are necessary preparations for inner illumination and relief.

8.

يَا أَيُّهَا الَّذِينَ آمَنُوا ادْخُلُوا فِي السِّلْمِ كَافَّةً وَلَا تَتَّبِعُوا خُطُوَاتِ الشَّيْطَانِ إِنَّهُ لَكُمْ عَدُوٌّ مُبِينٌ

O you who believe, enter Islam completely, and do not follow the bidding of *Shaytān*. Indeed, he is your open opponent.

2/208

9.

يَا أَيُّهَا الَّذِينَ آمَنُوا لِمَ تَقُولُونَ مَا لَا تَفْعَلُونَ

O you who believe, why do you say what you do not do?

61/2

Total obedience to the One Creator frees the wayfarer from the confusing demands of creation. If you cannot please Him, you will never be able to please others, and if you are pleasing to Him, then you do not need others. He is the evident Lord wherever you look, as well as the subtle hidden within you.

10.

وَيَسْتَعْجِلُونَكَ بِالْعَذَابِ وَلَوْلَا أَجَلٌ مُسَمًّى لَجَاءَهُمُ الْعَذَابُ وَلَيَأْتِيَنَّهُمْ بَغْتَةً وَهُمْ لَا يَشْعُرُونَ

They ask you hasten the punishment. If it were not a stipulated term, the punishment would have come to them already. It will come upon them suddenly when they are not expecting it.

Correct transactions and a proper relationship with creation are essential for spiritual progress. The truth is that all humankind has emerged from the one original primal self or soul. However, as individuals, we are different in terms of our looks, biology as well as states of consciousness and cultures.

Those who are free from the veils and darkness of the lower self are the ones who are free from the conflicting demands, desires and confusion.

11.

وَلَا تَنكِحُوا الْمُشْرِكَاتِ حَتَّىٰ يُؤْمِنَّ وَلَأَمَةٌ مُّؤْمِنَةٌ خَيْرٌ مِّن مُّشْرِكَةٍ وَلَوْ أَعْجَبَتْكُمْ وَلَا تُنكِحُوا الْمُشْرِكِينَ حَتَّىٰ يُؤْمِنُوا وَلَعَبْدٌ مُّؤْمِنٌ خَيْرٌ مِّن مُّشْرِكٍ وَلَوْ أَعْجَبَكُمْ أُولَٰئِكَ يَدْعُونَ إِلَى النَّارِ وَاللَّهُ يَدْعُو إِلَى الْجَنَّةِ وَالْمَغْفِرَةِ بِإِذْنِهِ وَيُبَيِّنُ آيَاتِهِ لِلنَّاسِ لَعَلَّهُمْ يَتَذَكَّرُونَ

Do not marry woman who associate (with Allah) until they believe. A believing slave-girl is better for you than a pagan woman though she may attract you. And do not marry men who associate (with Allah) until they believe, even though they may attract you. These people call you to hell whereas Allah calls you to paradise and forgiveness by His permission. He makes His signs clear to people so that hopefully they will pay heed

2/221

12.

ضَرَبَ اللَّهُ مَثَلًا عَبْدًا مَّمْلُوكًا لَّا يَقْدِرُ عَلَىٰ شَيْءٍ وَمَن رَّزَقْنَاهُ مِنَّا رِزْقًا حَسَنًا فَهُوَ يُنفِقُ مِنْهُ سِرًّا وَجَهْرًا هَلْ يَسْتَوُونَ الْحَمْدُ لِلَّهِ بَلْ أَكْثَرُهُمْ لَا يَعْلَمُونَ وَضَرَبَ اللَّهُ مَثَلًا رَّجُلَيْنِ أَحَدُهُمَا أَبْكَمُ لَا يَقْدِرُ عَلَىٰ شَيْءٍ وَهُوَ كَلٌّ عَلَىٰ مَوْلَاهُ أَيْنَمَا يُوَجِّههُّ لَا يَأْتِ بِخَيْرٍ هَلْ يَسْتَوِي هُوَ وَمَن يَأْمُرُ بِالْعَدْلِ وَهُوَ عَلَىٰ صِرَاطٍ مُّسْتَقِيمٍ

Allah strikes a metaphor (for you): Is an owned slave possessing no power the same as someone to whom We have given abundance and who gives from it secretly and openly? Praise be to Allah! But most people have no knowledge. Allah strikes (another) metaphor: two men, one of them dumb, unable to do anything, a burden to his master, no matter where he directs him, he brings no good; is he the same as someone who commands justice and is on a straight path?

16/75-76

13.

يَا أَيُّهَا الَّذِينَ آمَنُوا إِذَا نَكَحْتُمُ الْمُؤْمِنَاتِ ثُمَّ طَلَّقْتُمُوهُنَّ مِن قَبْلِ أَن تَمَسُّوهُنَّ فَمَا لَكُمْ عَلَيْهِنَّ مِنْ عِدَّةٍ تَعْتَدُّونَهَا فَمَتِّعُوهُنَّ وَسَرِّحُوهُنَّ سَرَاحًا جَمِيلًا

O you who believe, When you marry believing women and then divorce them before you have touched them, there is no waiting period (before they can marry again) for them. Act generously with them and let them, go with kindness.

33/49

14.

يَا أَيُّهَا الَّذِينَ آمَنُوا كُلُوا مِن طَيِّبَاتِ مَا رَزَقْنَاكُمْ وَاشْكُرُوا لِلَّهِ إِن كُنتُمْ إِيَّاهُ تَعْبُدُونَ إِنَّمَا حَرَّمَ عَلَيْكُمُ الْمَيْتَةَ وَالدَّمَ وَلَحْمَ الْخِنزِيرِ وَمَا أُهِلَّ بِهِ لِغَيْرِ اللَّهِ فَمَنِ اضْطُرَّ غَيْرَ بَاغٍ وَلَا عَادٍ فَلَا إِثْمَ عَلَيْهِ إِنَّ اللَّهَ غَفُورٌ رَّحِيمٌ

O you who believe, eat of the lawful things that we have provided for you, and give thanks to Allah if you worship Him alone. He has forbidden you stale, dead meat (carrion), blood, the flesh of swine, and that which has been sacrificed to other than Allah. But anyone who is driven by necessity to eat these – without desiring or eating excessively – commits no crime. Truly, Allah is Ever-Forgiving, Most Merciful.

2/172-173

15.

عَلَى الْكَافِرِينَ غَيْرُ يَسِيرٍ

There is anything but ease for the unbelievers.

74/10

Apart from the clearly restricted actions and prohibitions, there is much freedom of choice and many worldly pleasures that the seeker can enjoy. What we experience of this world is but a small sample or prelude of what is to come in the Hereafter. Outer forms perceived through the senses are only doors to meanings and the recognition of attributes. We realize that all worldly existence is founded on opposite qualities balancing each other and rooted in one other. The only constant reference point is the perfection of the One.

c. Supplications

Human nature is weak and in constant need of fulfillment and care. We also need steady guidance regarding the purpose and direction of life; thus the need for reference to Allah at all times, otherwise distractions will deflect us from the path.

1.

فَادْعُوا اللَّهَ مُخْلِصِينَ لَهُ الدِّينَ وَلَوْ كَرِهَ الْكَافِرُونَ

So call upon Allah, making your practice of his way pure, even though the forces of unbelief detest this.

40/14

2.

قَالَ رَبِّ اشْرَحْ لِي صَدْرِي

(Musa) said: O, my Lord, expand my heart.

20/25

3.

وَقُل رَّبِّ أَنزِلْنِي مُنزَلًا مُّبَارَكًا وَأَنتَ خَيْرُ الْمُنزِلِينَ

And say: My Lord, cause me to descend to a blessed landing-place. You are the best (for choosing) the place of descent.

23/29

These 'wayward' energies are ever present and can easily occupy any gap in our intentions and actions. Any 'vacancy' will inevitably be filled by seen or unseen entities or energies. Shaytān is the opposite and distant from Rahmān (the Merciful).

4.

وَقُل رَّبِّ أَعُوذُ بِكَ مِنْ هَمَزَاتِ الشَّيَاطِينِ

And say: My Lord, I seek refuge with You from the whispering of the evil ones.

23/97

5.

وَنَجِّنَا بِرَحْمَتِكَ مِنَ الْقَوْمِ الْكَافِرِينَ

And save us by Your mercy from the unbelievers.

10/86

The Religion (Dīn) c. Supplication

6.

قَدْ كَانَتْ لَكُمْ أُسْوَةٌ حَسَنَةٌ فِي إِبْرَاهِيمَ وَالَّذِينَ مَعَهُ إِذْ قَالُوا لِقَوْمِهِمْ إِنَّا بُرَآءُ مِنكُمْ وَمِمَّا تَعْبُدُونَ مِن دُونِ اللَّهِ كَفَرْنَا بِكُمْ وَبَدَا بَيْنَنَا وَبَيْنَكُمُ الْعَدَاوَةُ وَالْبَغْضَاءُ أَبَدًا حَتَّىٰ تُؤْمِنُوا بِاللَّهِ وَحْدَهُ إِلَّا قَوْلَ إِبْرَاهِيمَ لِأَبِيهِ لَأَسْتَغْفِرَنَّ لَكَ وَمَا أَمْلِكُ لَكَ مِنَ اللَّهِ مِن شَيْءٍ رَّبَّنَا عَلَيْكَ تَوَكَّلْنَا وَإِلَيْكَ أَنَبْنَا وَإِلَيْكَ الْمَصِيرُ

Indeed, you have an excellent example in Abraham and those with him, when they said to their people: We are free of you and all that you worship apart from Allah, and we reject you. Between us and you worship apart from Allah, and we reject you. Between us and you there will be enmity and hatred forever until you have faith in. Except for Abraham's word to his father: I will ask forgiveness for you, but I have no power to help you in any way against Allah. Our Lord, we have put our trust in You and have turned only *(tawbah)* to You. You are our final destination.

60/4

7.

رَبَّنَا اغْفِرْ لِي وَلِوَالِدَيَّ وَلِلْمُؤْمِنِينَ يَوْمَ يَقُومُ الْحِسَابُ

Our Lord! Forgive me and my parents and the believers on the Day when the Reckoning shall take place.

14/41

8.

رَبِّ اغْفِرْ لِي وَلِوَالِدَيَّ وَلِمَن دَخَلَ بَيْتِيَ مُؤْمِنًا وَلِلْمُؤْمِنِينَ وَالْمُؤْمِنَاتِ وَلَا تَزِدِ الظَّالِمِينَ إِلَّا تَبَارًا

My Lord, forgive me and my parents and all who enter my house as believers. And do not increase the wrongdoers except in ruin.

71/28

Mistakes and transgressions are part of the natural way of things. It is Allah's generosity that we recognize faults and seek remedies and corrections. This is an appropriate 'life transaction.'

The great Prophet Abraham was the best example of humble submission to his Lord whilst calling his people to the One and all controlling God. Abraham saw the transgressors as deviants and far from the ever-present mercy of Allah.

113

The prophetic qualities and conduct are a model for the seeker to copy and emulate. Our business in this life is to strive towards inner purification, clarity of intention and thereby access to His Light and Guidance. The prophets are the archetypal candles from which we can kindle ours.

Goodwill for parents and all creation frees the heart from the illusion and darkness of 'otherness' and negative emotions. When the heart is purified from all darkness shadows, it will overflow with the light of the soul, and thus will perceive the flickering worldly shadows with the right perspective.

Total reliance on Allah will free the seeker from expectation from His creation.

9.

قَالَ رَبِّ انصُرْنِي عَلَى الْقَوْمِ الْمُفْسِدِينَ

He said: My Lord, help me against the people of corruption.

29/30

10.

وَنَجِّنَا بِرَحْمَتِكَ مِنَ الْقَوْمِ الْكَافِرِينَ

And rescue us, by Your mercy, from the unbelieving people. And rescue us, by Your mercy, from the unbelieving people.

10/86

11.

رَبَّنَا لَا تُزِغْ قُلُوبَنَا بَعْدَ إِذْ هَدَيْتَنَا وَهَبْ لَنَا مِن لَّدُنكَ رَحْمَةً إِنَّكَ أَنتَ الْوَهَّابُ

Our Lord, do not cause our hearts to deviate after You have guided us. Grant us mercy from Your presence. Truly, You are the Bestower of all.

3/8

12.

وَمَا كَانَ قَوْلَهُمْ إِلَّا أَن قَالُوا رَبَّنَا اغْفِرْ لَنَا ذُنُوبَنَا وَإِسْرَافَنَا فِي أَمْرِنَا وَثَبِّتْ أَقْدَامَنَا وَانصُرْنَا عَلَى الْقَوْمِ الْكَافِرِينَ

All they said was: Our Lord, forgive our mistakes and transgressions, establish our feet firmly, and grant us victory over the unbelievers.

3/147

13.

قَالَ كَلَّا إِنَّ مَعِيَ رَبِّي سَيَهْدِينِ

He said: Never! My Lord is with me and He will guide me.

26/62

14.

وَلَمَّا بَرَزُوا لِجَالُوتَ وَجُنُودِهِ قَالُوا رَبَّنَا أَفْرِغْ عَلَيْنَا صَبْرًا وَثَبِّتْ أَقْدَامَنَا وَانصُرْنَا عَلَى الْقَوْمِ الْكَافِرِينَ

And when they advanced to meet Goliath and his forces, they said: Our Lord! Pour forth on us patience, set firmly our feet, and make us victorious over these unbelievers.

2/250

15.

فَأَقِمْ وَجْهَكَ لِلدِّينِ حَنِيفًا فِطْرَتَ اللَّهِ الَّتِي فَطَرَ النَّاسَ عَلَيْهَا لَا تَبْدِيلَ لِخَلْقِ اللَّهِ ذَٰلِكَ الدِّينُ الْقَيِّمُ وَلَٰكِنَّ أَكْثَرَ النَّاسِ لَا يَعْلَمُونَ

So set yourself firmly on the most natural path of (worshiping) Allah. (This is) Allah's original primal pattern on which He created mankind. There is no changing Allah's creation. That is the true path of Allah, but most of mankind has no knowledge.

30/30

16.

رَبَّنَا وَاجْعَلْنَا مُسْلِمَيْنِ لَكَ وَمِن ذُرِّيَّتِنَا أُمَّةً مُّسْلِمَةً لَّكَ وَأَرِنَا مَنَاسِكَنَا وَتُبْ عَلَيْنَا إِنَّكَ أَنتَ التَّوَّابُ الرَّحِيمُ

Our Lord, grant us unconditional surrender to You, and (make) our descendants a community submitted to You. Show us our rites of worship and turn towards us. Truly, You are the Oft-Returning, the Most Merciful.

2/128

17.

وَقُل رَّبِّ أَدْخِلْنِي مُدْخَلَ صِدْقٍ وَأَخْرِجْنِي مُخْرَجَ صِدْقٍ وَاجْعَل لِّي مِن لَّدُنكَ سُلْطَانًا نَّصِيرًا

Say: My Lord, make my entry sincere and make my leaving sincere; and grant me a supporting authority directly from Your presence.

17/80

18.

وَقُل رَّبِّ اغْفِرْ وَارْحَمْ وَأَنتَ خَيْرُ الرَّاحِمِينَ

Say: My Lord, forgive and be merciful! You are the best of the Merciful.

23/118

Human nature is such that we will commit mistakes and wrong actions so that we are humbled and moved to call upon the All-Knowing, All-Forgiving and Ever-Present. His glorious Attributes can cover our vices when we call upon Him with sincerity and repentance. To witness Him we must turn away from the distractions and illusions of shadows.

What matters is our regret for wrong actions and awareness of His mercy. Our resolve not to repeat a mistake comes about through responsible focused intentions, constancy and love for His perfections.

Beginning with the admission of human weakness, our submission will bring about His gifts of mercy and strength. The path will enable the seeker to replace self-concern with knowledge of His concern.

CHAPTER NINE

THE ADAMIC SELF

The Qur'an gives us a challenging description of the Adamic potential and levels of consciousness. The human quest is symbolized by the descent of Adam to earth. Allah describes the primal dramatic events as a prelude leading to knowledge of the Creator through submission, knowledge and transformative worship.

There is one original blueprint of the human self from which all selves have come. The forces of attraction and repulsion drive the human self towards many levels of fulfillment. Destiny is determined by the decrees, laws and patterns, which govern existence. If we submit and aspire to the higher and act appropriately, we will awaken to realities and knowledge leading us to the ultimate truth. On the other hand, if we fall into the pitfalls of the lower self, then disillusionment and confusion will ensue. Human awareness of the lower tendencies is the driving force towards higher attributes and values, which are latent in us.

The number and types of seekers of truth, their colour or culture, is beyond count, yet their destination is one. The determined ones, who serve in the way of Truth and who transcend the lower self, will reach their destination successfully. The lower self seeks ease, pleasure and power. Once a being is illumined with the knowledge of the All-Encompassing God, His unity, His ever-presence and His dominance, then these lower tendencies are treated and checked and gradually replaced by illumination, inner light and witnessing.

Every human being seeks a destiny of durable inner contentment, peace and happiness. The path to this end is that of submission (*islam*) while the driving force is faith (*imān*). The perfection of this transformation is faultless and pure transaction (*ihsān*).

The Prophet has said that he who knows himself knows his Lord. Knowledge of self, therefore, is the foundation of spiritual progress and knowledge. The human self belongs to the realm of subtle entities and lights. It is a divine entity, energized by the spirit (*rūh*) while interacting with physical matter. The self relates to the body and the senses and brings them to life, whereas its root and essence is the spirit. It is an interspace and a bridge between this world and the world of the unseen. As the essential nature of the self is spiritual light, it yearns constantly for the perfect and boundless realm of non-time and non-space.

In childhood, the self is preoccupied with nurturing the young body and developing its physiology and senses. But with age, experience and the development of the cognitive faculty, the self looks for nourishment and guidance from the intellect and from the spirit. It moves from total identification with the body and the world of physicality and the senses to concern for meanings and higher, subtler qualities. Love of beautiful objects would thus lead to love of the ideal of beauty and then love for the Source of all beauty.

It is essential for the seeker of self-knowledge to acquire modesty, courage, wisdom and justice. When the self is groomed, and the natural, early vices have been checked and replaced with virtues that become the new habits, then it becomes clear that the inherent drive is towards Allah's perfect Attributes. Because the lower self has been superseded, the higher self will simply reflect the essential qualities of generosity, mercy, forbearance, forgiveness, modesty, patience, knowledge, and piety.

The Adamic self belongs to the Eternal Garden and its struggle in this world is to recognize the undesirable tendencies and turn towards the higher virtuous qualities that will then envelope it. Through the discriminative capacity of the intellect the self will realize that its true love is that of meaning and essence, so its focus shifts from ever-changing darkness and shadows to light, clarity and reliable inner reference. This is the goal and the state of self-knowledge and enlightenment.

The Adamic Self

1.

وَإِذْ قَالَ رَبُّكَ لِلْمَلَائِكَةِ إِنِّي جَاعِلٌ فِي الْأَرْضِ خَلِيفَةً قَالُوا أَتَجْعَلُ فِيهَا مَن يُفْسِدُ فِيهَا وَيَسْفِكُ الدِّمَاءَ وَنَحْنُ نُسَبِّحُ بِحَمْدِكَ وَنُقَدِّسُ لَكَ قَالَ إِنِّي أَعْلَمُ مَا لَا تَعْلَمُونَ

When your Lord said to the angels: I am putting a vicegerent on the Earth, they said: Will you place in it one who will cause corruption and shed blood, While we glorify You with praise and proclaim Your sanctity? He said: I know what you do not know.

2/30

2.

وَقُلْنَا يَا آدَمُ اسْكُنْ أَنتَ وَزَوْجُكَ الْجَنَّةَ وَكُلَا مِنْهَا رَغَدًا حَيْثُ شِئْتُمَا وَلَا تَقْرَبَا هَٰذِهِ الشَّجَرَةَ فَتَكُونَا مِنَ الظَّالِمِينَ

We said: O Adam, live in the Garden you and your wife, and eat freely from it wherever you will. But do not approach this tree and so become wrongdoers.

2/35

3.

يَا بَنِي آدَمَ لَا يَفْتِنَنَّكُمُ الشَّيْطَانُ كَمَا أَخْرَجَ أَبَوَيْكُم مِّنَ الْجَنَّةِ يَنزِعُ عَنْهُمَا لِبَاسَهُمَا لِيُرِيَهُمَا سَوْآتِهِمَا إِنَّهُ يَرَاكُمْ هُوَ وَقَبِيلُهُ مِنْ حَيْثُ لَا تَرَوْنَهُمْ إِنَّا جَعَلْنَا الشَّيَاطِينَ أَوْلِيَاءَ لِلَّذِينَ لَا يُؤْمِنُونَ

O Children of Adam, do not let *Shaytān* captivate you with temptations and subject you to trials as he caused the expulsion of your parents from the Garden, stripping them of their covering and disclosing to them their shame. He and his tribe see you from where you do not see them. We have made the *shaytāns* friends of those who have no faith.

7/27

Self-consciousness arose within the Adamic being which was born in the perfect paradise. He descended to earthly experience in order to regain his original heritage 'by choice'. Thus Adam was given the highest honour in this choice. Man will experience doubt, uncertainty and fears whilst returning to the certainty of knowledge and light which envelops all existence.

The Adamic desire or concern for provision arose as a Shaytānic disturbance. On earth Adam has the responsibility with the choice between good and evil, acceptance and rejection, sustained joy and short-lived pleasure, truth and falsehood, self-reliance or God-dependence. These opposites constitute the foundations of worldly experiences.

The ultimate human pursuit relates to knowledge of His ever-present Light, which permeates all creations in existence and gives them their appropriate identities and realities. In the presence of His permanent Light, everything in existence is temporary, dependent on Him. Thus solid mountains will declare their weakness, or fluidity. Once seen with the eye of truth they move and change like clouds.

Whilst the human form is composed of earthly matter, its roots and origins are heavenly.

All creation desires eternal harmony and contentment, which are imprinted upon the soul. These qualities belong to the next world but are only reflected in the ever-changing world of materiality.

4.

وَلَقَدْ خَلَقْنَا الْإِنسَانَ وَنَعْلَمُ مَا تُوَسْوِسُ بِهِ نَفْسُهُ وَنَحْنُ أَقْرَبُ إِلَيْهِ مِنْ حَبْلِ الْوَرِيدِ

Indeed, We have created man, and We know the silent discourse of his soul, what his own self whispers to him. We are nearer to him than his jugular vein.

50/16

5.

إِنَّا عَرَضْنَا الْأَمَانَةَ عَلَى السَّمَاوَاتِ وَالْأَرْضِ وَالْجِبَالِ فَأَبَيْنَ أَن يَحْمِلْنَهَا وَأَشْفَقْنَ مِنْهَا وَحَمَلَهَا الْإِنسَانُ إِنَّهُ كَانَ ظَلُومًا جَهُولًا

Truly, We offered the trust to the heavens and the earth, and to the mountains, but they declined to assume it and shrank from it; but man took it on. Surely, he (despite this divine trust) is oppressive and ignorant.

33/72

6.

وَلَقَدْ خَلَقْنَا الْإِنسَانَ مِن سُلَالَةٍ مِّن طِينٍ ثُمَّ جَعَلْنَاهُ نُطْفَةً فِي قَرَارٍ مَّكِينٍ ثُمَّ خَلَقْنَا النُّطْفَةَ عَلَقَةً فَخَلَقْنَا الْعَلَقَةَ مُضْغَةً فَخَلَقْنَا الْمُضْغَةَ عِظَامًا فَكَسَوْنَا الْعِظَامَ لَحْمًا ثُمَّ أَنشَأْنَاهُ خَلْقًا آخَرَ فَتَبَارَكَ اللَّهُ أَحْسَنُ الْخَالِقِينَ ثُمَّ إِنَّكُم بَعْدَ ذَلِكَ لَمَيِّتُونَ ثُمَّ إِنَّكُمْ يَوْمَ الْقِيَامَةِ تُبْعَثُونَ

Truly, We created man as an extract from the composition of earthly elements (clay); Then placed him as a drop (of seed) in a secure receptacle; Then formed the drop into a clot, and formed the clot into a lump, and formed the lump into bones, and clothed the bones in flesh. Then we brought him into being as another creation. Blessed be Allah, the Best of Creators! Then subsequently you will die. On the Day of Rising you will be raised again.

23/12-16

The Adamic Self

7.

إِنَّ ٱلْإِنسَٰنَ خُلِقَ هَلُوعًا ۝ إِذَا مَسَّهُ ٱلشَّرُّ جَزُوعًا ۝ وَإِذَا مَسَّهُ ٱلْخَيْرُ مَنُوعًا ۝ إِلَّا ٱلْمُصَلِّينَ ۝ ٱلَّذِينَ هُمْ عَلَىٰ صَلَاتِهِمْ دَآئِمُونَ ۝ وَٱلَّذِينَ فِىٓ أَمْوَٰلِهِمْ حَقٌّ مَّعْلُومٌ ۝ لِّلسَّآئِلِ وَٱلْمَحْرُومِ ۝ وَٱلَّذِينَ يُصَدِّقُونَ بِيَوْمِ ٱلدِّينِ ۝ وَٱلَّذِينَ هُم مِّنْ عَذَابِ رَبِّهِم مُّشْفِقُونَ ۝ إِنَّ عَذَابَ رَبِّهِمْ غَيْرُ مَأْمُونٍ ۝

Truly man was created of a hasty temperament, headstrong Desperate and anxious when bad things happen, begrudging when good things come to him – except those who are devoted to prayer, those who remain constant in it; And those in whose wealth there is a recognizable share for the beggars and the destitute; And those who accept the truth of the judgment day fearing the punishment of their Lord. Truly, no one should feel secure from the chastisement of his Lord.

70/19-28

8.

لَقَدْ خَلَقْنَا ٱلْإِنسَٰنَ فِى كَبَدٍ

Truly, We have created man in toil.

90/4

9.

إِنَّ ٱلْإِنسَٰنَ لِرَبِّهِۦ لَكَنُودٌ

Truly, man is ungrateful to his Lord.

100/6

10.

يَٰٓأَيُّهَا ٱلْإِنسَٰنُ إِنَّكَ كَادِحٌ إِلَىٰ رَبِّكَ كَدْحًا فَمُلَٰقِيهِ

O man, you are toiling laboriously towards your Lord so you will meet Him.

84/6

The selfish, childish and immature lower nature of man is mainly concerned with physical preservation, which is the nature of the vegetative and animal self. With healthy development and discrimination, the concern for meaning and essence will increase. Higher consciousness and reflection allow man to rise to the station of divine vicegerency on earth. This illumination is balanced by accountability to Him with every breath and movement.

Remembrance and reference to Allah tethers the self and revives the seeker in this time/space confinement with increased yearning for perfection. The awakened self simply receives the heavenly lights and patterns from the spirit (rūh).

The nature of the lower self is doubt and disobedience whilst developing and striving for the divine qualities and perfection of cognition.

The design and pattern within all souls is essentially one in origin. This divinely entity contains within it all the creational designs, frequencies and realities.

The human self contains within it tendencies which relate to both its celestial origin as well as its temporary terrestrial connections. This world is the action zone that prepares the self for awakening to the everlasting reality of the rūh or soul. This enlightened awakening is the natural destination for the self.

11.

يُرِيدُ اللَّهُ أَن يُخَفِّفَ عَنكُمْ وَخُلِقَ الْإِنسَانُ ضَعِيفًا

Allah desires to make things lighter for you. Man was created weak.

4/28

12.

وَلَا أُقْسِمُ بِالنَّفْسِ اللَّوَّامَةِ

Nay! I swear by the self-reproaching soul (nafs).

75/2

13.

يَا أَيُّهَا النَّاسُ اتَّقُوا رَبَّكُمُ الَّذِي خَلَقَكُم مِّن نَّفْسٍ وَاحِدَةٍ وَخَلَقَ مِنْهَا زَوْجَهَا وَبَثَّ مِنْهُمَا رِجَالًا كَثِيرًا وَنِسَاءً وَاتَّقُوا اللَّهَ الَّذِي تَسَاءَلُونَ بِهِ وَالْأَرْحَامَ إِنَّ اللَّهَ كَانَ عَلَيْكُمْ رَقِيبًا

O mankind! Be cautiously aware of your Lord who created you from a single self and created its mate from it, and from them both He spread forth many men and women. Have awareness of Allah in whose name you make demands on one another and also in respect of your families. Allah watches over you continually.

1/4

14.

زُيِّنَ لِلنَّاسِ حُبُّ الشَّهَوَاتِ مِنَ النِّسَاءِ وَالْبَنِينَ وَالْقَنَاطِيرِ الْمُقَنطَرَةِ مِنَ الذَّهَبِ وَالْفِضَّةِ وَالْخَيْلِ الْمُسَوَّمَةِ وَالْأَنْعَامِ وَالْحَرْثِ ذَٰلِكَ مَتَاعُ الْحَيَاةِ الدُّنْيَا وَاللَّهُ عِندَهُ حُسْنُ الْمَآبِ

Beautiful for mankind is the love of desires for women, children, accumulated wealth of gold and silver, horses with fine markings, livestock and fertile farmland. All that is merely the enjoyment of the life of the world, while with Allah is the best abode.

3/14

15.

وَلَا يَحْسَبَنَّ الَّذِينَ يَبْخَلُونَ بِمَا آتَاهُمُ اللَّهُ مِن فَضْلِهِ هُوَ خَيْرًا لَّهُم ۖ بَلْ هُوَ شَرٌّ لَّهُمْ ۖ سَيُطَوَّقُونَ مَا بَخِلُوا بِهِ يَوْمَ الْقِيَامَةِ ۗ وَلِلَّهِ مِيرَاثُ السَّمَاوَاتِ وَالْأَرْضِ ۗ وَاللَّهُ بِمَا تَعْمَلُونَ خَبِيرٌ

Do not let those who covetously withhold that which Allah has bestowed on them of His bounty think that it is better for them. Indeed, it is worse for them. That which they hoard will tightly enclose them like a collar on the Day of Resurrection. Allah is the inheritor of the heavens and the earth, and Allah is aware of what you do.

3/180

16.

كُلُّ نَفْسٍ ذَائِقَةُ الْمَوْتِ ۗ وَإِنَّمَا تُوَفَّوْنَ أُجُورَكُمْ يَوْمَ الْقِيَامَةِ ۖ فَمَن زُحْزِحَ عَنِ النَّارِ وَأُدْخِلَ الْجَنَّةَ فَقَدْ فَازَ ۗ وَمَا الْحَيَاةُ الدُّنْيَا إِلَّا مَتَاعُ الْغُرُورِ

Every self will taste death. You will be fully compensated on the Day of Rising. Whoever is distanced from hell fire and admitted to the Garden has triumphed. The life of the world (*dunya*) is nothing but an illusory enjoyment.

3/185

17.

فَمَن يَعْمَلْ مِثْقَالَ ذَرَّةٍ خَيْرًا يَرَهُ وَمَن يَعْمَلْ مِثْقَالَ ذَرَّةٍ شَرًّا يَرَهُ

Whoever does an atom's weight of good will see it, And whoever does an atom's weight of evil will see it.

99/7-8

18.

مَّن جَاءَ بِالْحَسَنَةِ فَلَهُ عَشْرُ أَمْثَالِهَا ۖ وَمَن جَاءَ بِالسَّيِّئَةِ فَلَا يُجْزَىٰ إِلَّا مِثْلَهَا وَهُمْ لَا يُظْلَمُونَ

Those who produce a good action will receive ten like it. But those who produce a bad action will be repaid by its equivalent, and they will not be wronged.

6/160

The Hereafter is non-time/space sphere of existence, thus it is forever. The self shall experience the next life according to its levels or states of perfection or otherwise in its life.

Departure from this world is the most certain event and remembrance of this threshold event will enhance Transformation of consciousness.

In this world, all actions and intentions affect the self by increasing or reducing its veils from the spirit (*the rūh*), which is its energizer source and container of the original divine code and truth,

Since every action impacts upon the self, constant vigilance, awareness and accountability are necessary keys to open the heart and inner eye to His perfect designs.

Since the world of time/space is but a flicker in relation to eternity, the latter is nearer than we can imagine. The rūh is not of this world and recognizes this truth, whereas the self relates to the rūh through the physical world.

At the human level, we try to preserve, perpetuate and attract what is desirable and repel what we perceive as undesirable. All human drives depend upon attraction or repulsion: drawing near to what the self seeks or avoiding what it dislikes.

Allah's design is such that every creation looks for its perfect origin or source and as such is stimulated by the love of the higher and subtler, the vast unseen world.

19.

وَأَقِيمُوا۟ ٱلصَّلَوٰةَ وَءَاتُوا۟ ٱلزَّكَوٰةَ وَمَا تُقَدِّمُوا۟ لِأَنفُسِكُم مِّنْ خَيْرٍ تَجِدُوهُ عِندَ ٱللَّهِ إِنَّ ٱللَّهَ بِمَا تَعْمَلُونَ بَصِيرٌ

Whatever good you send forth for yourselves, you will find it with Allah. Surely Allah is the Seer of what you do.

2/110

20.

ٱقْتَرَبَ لِلنَّاسِ حِسَابُهُمْ وَهُمْ فِى غَفْلَةٍ مُّعْرِضُونَ مَا يَأْتِيهِم مِّن ذِكْرٍ مِّن رَّبِّهِم مُّحْدَثٍ إِلَّا ٱسْتَمَعُوهُ وَهُمْ يَلْعَبُونَ

Man's reckoning draws very close, yet he heedlessly turns away. Every fresh reminder of their Lord that comes to them goes unheeded as if they were playing a game.

21/1-2

21.

كُلُّ نَفْسٍۭ بِمَا كَسَبَتْ رَهِينَةٌ

Every self is held in pledge against what it earned.

74/38

22.

فَإِنْ أَعْرَضُوا۟ فَمَآ أَرْسَلْنَٰكَ عَلَيْهِمْ حَفِيظًا إِنْ عَلَيْكَ إِلَّا ٱلْبَلَٰغُ وَإِنَّآ إِذَآ أَذَقْنَا ٱلْإِنسَٰنَ مِنَّا رَحْمَةً فَرِحَ بِهَا وَإِن تُصِبْهُمْ سَيِّئَةٌۢ بِمَا قَدَّمَتْ أَيْدِيهِمْ فَإِنَّ ٱلْإِنسَٰنَ كَفُورٌ

But if they turn away, We have not sent you to be their guardian. You are only responsible for transmission. When We let a man experience mercy from Us he exults in it. And if something bad befalls him because of what he has done, he is ungrateful.

42/48

23.

وَلَئِنْ أَذَقْنَا الْإِنسَانَ مِنَّا رَحْمَةً ثُمَّ نَزَعْنَاهَا مِنْهُ إِنَّهُ لَيَئُوسٌ كَفُورٌ ۝ وَلَئِنْ أَذَقْنَاهُ نَعْمَاءَ بَعْدَ ضَرَّاءَ مَسَّتْهُ لَيَقُولَنَّ ذَهَبَ السَّيِّئَاتُ عَنِّي إِنَّهُ لَفَرِحٌ فَخُورٌ ۝ إِلَّا الَّذِينَ صَبَرُوا وَعَمِلُوا الصَّالِحَاتِ أُولَٰئِكَ لَهُم مَّغْفِرَةٌ وَأَجْرٌ كَبِيرٌ

If We let man experience mercy from Us, and then take it away from him, he is despairing, ungrateful; But if We let him experience blessings after hardship has afflicted him, he says: My troubles have gone away, and he is overjoyed, boastful; Except for those who are steadfast and perform right actions. They will receive forgiveness and a large reward.

11/9-11

24.

وَلَقَدْ صَرَّفْنَا فِي هَٰذَا الْقُرْآنِ لِلنَّاسِ مِن كُلِّ مَثَلٍ وَكَانَ الْإِنسَانُ أَكْثَرَ شَيْءٍ جَدَلًا

We have detailed throughout this Qur'an many examples for people, but, above anything else, man is contentious.

18/54

25.

وَوَصَّيْنَا الْإِنسَانَ بِوَالِدَيْهِ حُسْنًا وَإِن جَاهَدَاكَ لِتُشْرِكَ بِي مَا لَيْسَ لَكَ بِهِ عِلْمٌ فَلَا تُطِعْهُمَا إِلَيَّ مَرْجِعُكُمْ فَأُنَبِّئُكُم بِمَا كُنتُمْ تَعْمَلُونَ

We have enjoined upon man to be kind and dutiful to his parents; but if they strive to make you associate with Me anything that you have no knowledge of, then do not obey them. Unto Me is your return, and I shall inform you of your actions.

29/8

Patience ultimately means going beyond the boundaries of time. Allah is the ever patient in that He is beyond time. Qur'an gives to us the keys and doors to all the archetypes, original patterns, decrees and holographic paradigms of manifestation.

The quality of a human being is ultimately dependent on the quality of one's heart and its illumination, not what appears as pleasant and appealing as outer manners. Like clothes, these can hide many faults. The illumined pure heart overflows in contentment with His Love and proximity.

Peace can only be preserved by willingness to fight injustice and ignorance. What we always seek is durable and reliable goodness and happiness. Life is balanced by denial of evil and assertion of virtue. If we perform our duty properly then access to inspiration and creativity will naturally occur.

26.

وَمِنَ ٱلنَّاسِ مَن يُعْجِبُكَ قَوْلُهُ فِى ٱلْحَيَوٰةِ ٱلدُّنْيَا وَيُشْهِدُ ٱللَّهَ عَلَىٰ مَا فِى قَلْبِهِ وَهُوَ أَلَدُّ ٱلْخِصَامِ

Among people there is the one whose words about the life of this world excite your imagination. He calls Allah to witness what is in his heart, while he is in fact the most hostile of adversaries.

2/204

27.

إِنَّ ٱللَّهَ عِندَهُ عِلْمُ ٱلسَّاعَةِ وَيُنَزِّلُ ٱلْغَيْثَ وَيَعْلَمُ مَا فِى ٱلْأَرْحَامِ وَمَا تَدْرِى نَفْسٌ مَّاذَا تَكْسِبُ غَدًا وَمَا تَدْرِى نَفْسٌ بِأَىِّ أَرْضٍ تَمُوتُ إِنَّ ٱللَّهَ عَلِيمٌ خَبِيرٌ

Surely, Allah has knowledge of the Hour. He sends down abundant rain, and He knows what is in the wombs. No self knows what it will earn tomorrow, and no self knows in what land it will die. Allah is All-Knowing, All-Aware.

31/34

28.

كُتِبَ عَلَيْكُمُ ٱلْقِتَالُ وَهُوَ كُرْهٌ لَّكُمْ وَعَسَىٰ أَن تَكْرَهُوا شَيْئًا وَهُوَ خَيْرٌ لَّكُمْ وَعَسَىٰ أَن تُحِبُّوا شَيْئًا وَهُوَ شَرٌّ لَّكُمْ وَٱللَّهُ يَعْلَمُ وَأَنتُمْ لَا تَعْلَمُونَ

Fighting is prescribed for you even though it is hateful to you. It may be that you dislike something when it is good for you, and it may be that you love something when it is bad for you. Allah knows, and you do not know.

2/216

29.

يَا أَيَّتُهَا النَّفْسُ الْمُطْمَئِنَّةُ ارْجِعِي إِلَىٰ رَبِّكِ رَاضِيَةً مَّرْضِيَّةً فَادْخُلِي فِي عِبَادِي وَادْخُلِي جَنَّتِي

O soul at rest and at peace, Return to your Lord, well pleasing and well pleased. Come to me as a true worshipper, And enter My paradise.

89/27-30

30.

بَلِ الْإِنسَانُ عَلَىٰ نَفْسِهِ بَصِيرَةٌ وَلَوْ أَلْقَىٰ مَعَاذِيرَهُ

Man is a clear witness against himself, though he may offer an excuse.

75/14-15

31.

أَلَّا تَزِرُ وَازِرَةٌ وِزْرَ أُخْرَىٰ وَأَن لَّيْسَ لِلْإِنسَانِ إِلَّا مَا سَعَىٰ وَأَنَّ سَعْيَهُ سَوْفَ يُرَىٰ ثُمَّ يُجْزَاهُ الْجَزَاءَ الْأَوْفَىٰ وَأَنَّ إِلَىٰ رَبِّكَ الْمُنتَهَىٰ

No one shall bear another's burden, And man will have only what he strives for. His striving will most certainly be seen, and then he will receive payment in full. Verily, the ultimate end is with your Lord.

53/38-42

32.

قُلْ يَا أَيُّهَا النَّاسُ قَدْ جَاءَكُمُ الْحَقُّ مِن رَّبِّكُمْ فَمَنِ اهْتَدَىٰ فَإِنَّمَا يَهْتَدِي لِنَفْسِهِ وَمَن ضَلَّ فَإِنَّمَا يَضِلُّ عَلَيْهَا وَمَا أَنَا عَلَيْكُم بِوَكِيلٍ

Say: O mankind! The truth has come to you from your Lord. Whoever is guided, is only guided for his own good, and whoever goes astray is only misguided to his detriment. I have not been set over you as a guardian.

10/108

It is only the contented self that can ascend to its source and its divine origin. That is the zone of real joy without interruption.

The self has within it a witnessing capacity that reveals the reality of a situation. When this reference point is relied upon, real progress towards awakening witnessing of truth will occur.

Everyone's experience is according to his or her direction and objectives. The seeker of truth will eventually witness His pervasiveness and Presence and thus become content at heart beyond any doubt that the most Generous and Just Lord is in charge of all situations and at all times.

To be well guided is a natural tendency of the healthy self. However, when we fall into the pitfalls of the lower self and its desires and veils, ignorance becomes acceptable and the perceived norm.

Every self in this world is writing its future by what it does and pursues. Those who seek knowledge of Him will attain it. And those who are at a loss and justify their wrong actions will also experience confusion and disappointment.

Indeed, the entire purpose of creation is to know and adore Him, the most Glorious and Perfect Lord of existence. The self loves itself until it realizes that at the very least it is reflecting aspects of Divine qualities. Thus its true love begins to be discovered by the soul within.

33.

وَمِنَ النَّاسِ وَالدَّوَابِّ وَالْأَنْعَامِ مُخْتَلِفٌ أَلْوَانُهُ كَذَٰلِكَ إِنَّمَا يَخْشَى اللَّهَ مِنْ عِبَادِهِ الْعُلَمَاءُ إِنَّ اللَّهَ عَزِيزٌ غَفُورٌ

Amongst mankind, beasts and livestock are varying types and species. Only those of His slaves with knowledge have fear of Allah. Allah is Almighty, Ever-Forgiving.

35/28

34.

قُلْ أَغَيْرَ اللَّهِ أَبْغِي رَبًّا وَهُوَ رَبُّ كُلِّ شَيْءٍ وَلَا تَكْسِبُ كُلُّ نَفْسٍ إِلَّا عَلَيْهَا وَلَا تَزِرُ وَازِرَةٌ وِزْرَ أُخْرَىٰ ثُمَّ إِلَىٰ رَبِّكُمْ مَرْجِعُكُمْ فَيُنَبِّئُكُمْ بِمَا كُنْتُمْ فِيهِ تَخْتَلِفُونَ

Say: Shall I desire any other than Allah as Lord when He is the Lord of all things? What each self earns is for itself alone. No one can bear another's burden. Then you will return to your Lord, and He will inform you regarding the things about which you differed.

6/164

35.

وَهُوَ الَّذِي سَخَّرَ الْبَحْرَ لِتَأْكُلُوا مِنْهُ لَحْمًا طَرِيًّا وَتَسْتَخْرِجُوا مِنْهُ حِلْيَةً تَلْبَسُونَهَا وَتَرَى الْفُلْكَ مَوَاخِرَ فِيهِ وَلِتَبْتَغُوا مِنْ فَضْلِهِ وَلَعَلَّكُمْ تَشْكُرُونَ

It is He who made the sea subservient to you so that you may eat the fresh flesh from it and bring out from it ornaments to wear. And you see the ships cleaving through it so that you may seek His bounty, and so that hopefully you will be thankful.

16/14

The Adamic Self

36.

مَا جَعَلَ ٱللَّهُ لِرَجُلٍ مِّن قَلْبَيْنِ فِى جَوْفِهِۦ ۚ وَمَا جَعَلَ أَزْوَٰجَكُمُ ٱلَّٰٓـِٔى تُظَٰهِرُونَ مِنْهُنَّ أُمَّهَٰتِكُمْ ۚ وَمَا جَعَلَ أَدْعِيَآءَكُمْ أَبْنَآءَكُمْ ۚ ذَٰلِكُمْ قَوْلُكُم بِأَفْوَٰهِكُمْ ۖ وَٱللَّهُ يَقُولُ ٱلْحَقَّ وَهُوَ يَهْدِى ٱلسَّبِيلَ

Allah has not made for any man two hearts inside his body. Neither has He made your wives whom you declare to be like your mother's back, your real mother. Nor has He made your adopted sons your real sons. That is but your saying with your mouths. But Allah speaks the truth,
and He guides you to the Way.

33/4

37.

كُلُّ نَفْسٍ ذَآئِقَةُ ٱلْمَوْتِ ۗ وَنَبْلُوكُم بِٱلشَّرِّ وَٱلْخَيْرِ فِتْنَةً ۖ وَإِلَيْنَا تُرْجَعُونَ

Every self shall taste death. We test you with both good and evil as a trial. And to us you will be returned.

21/35

38.

إِنَّا هَدَيْنَٰهُ ٱلسَّبِيلَ إِمَّا شَاكِرًا وَإِمَّا كَفُورًا

Surely we guide him to the way, whether he is grateful or ungrateful.

76/3

39.

مَّآ أَصَابَكَ مِنْ حَسَنَةٍ فَمِنَ ٱللَّهِ ۖ وَمَآ أَصَابَكَ مِن سَيِّئَةٍ فَمِن نَّفْسِكَ ۚ وَأَرْسَلْنَٰكَ لِلنَّاسِ رَسُولًا ۚ وَكَفَىٰ بِٱللَّهِ شَهِيدًا

Whatever good you experience is from Allah, and whatever bad befalls you is from yourself. We have sent you to mankind as a Messenger. Allah suffices as a Witness.

4/79

At any given moment we can only follow one direction or intention. This action is either towards the higher with effort, or towards the lower with apparent ease. We can only shoot one arrow at a time from the bow, well with care, or badly with ignorance.

The path is either towards illumination and knowledge that leads to contentment and gratitude or towards increased pursuit of pleasure, self-gratification, and subsequent disappointment and grief.

All goodness emanates from the higher self or soul whereas evil is the tendency of the lower self. When the self is truly harnessed through vigilant awareness, the inner light will lead to the abode of perfection.

Besides the powers of attraction and repulsion within the self, there are cognitive, witnessing and self-monitoring domains, within the heart. It is through a purified heart that these higher facets of consciousness are developed.

The nature of the lower self is always weak and unreliable. It is only when groomed through dedicated service and illumined faith and patience that the human self can be raised to reflect the divine spirit. Then it has fulfilled its potential and purpose.

40.

وَمَا أُبَرِّئُ نَفْسِي إِنَّ ٱلنَّفْسَ لَأَمَّارَةٌ بِٱلسُّوٓءِ إِلَّا مَا رَحِمَ رَبِّىٓ إِنَّ رَبِّى غَفُورٌ رَّحِيمٌ

I do not absolve myself (from blame). Most surely the self commands to evil acts, except for those my Lord has mercy upon. My Lord is Forgiving, Merciful.

12/53

41.

إِن كُلُّ نَفْسٍ لَّمَّا عَلَيْهَا حَافِظٌ

Every self (soul) has a guardian over it.

86/4

42.

وَجَآءَتْ كُلُّ نَفْسٍ مَّعَهَا سَآئِقٌ وَشَهِيدٌ

Every soul occurs with a driver and a witness.

50/21

43.

وَٱلْعَصْرِ
إِنَّ ٱلْإِنسَانَ لَفِي خُسْرٍ
إِلَّا ٱلَّذِينَ ءَامَنُوا۟ وَعَمِلُوا۟ ٱلصَّالِحَاتِ وَتَوَاصَوْا۟ بِٱلْحَقِّ وَتَوَاصَوْا۟ بِٱلصَّبْرِ

Throughout time, Man is most surely in a state of loss, Except for those who have faith, do right actions, and urge each other to the truth and to steadfastness.

103/1-3

NATIONS AND CULTURES

A society is an aggregate of individuals interacting and influencing each other within cultural norms and customs. The styles, habits and physical aspects of a culture are naturally influenced by its history, geography, environment and socio-economic factors. The state of a people is a function of many complex exogenous and endogenous influences. The rise and fall of nations and people is highly dependent on the presence and absence of durable qualities such as ethics, morality, and justice. The presence of these qualities ensures the wisdom of its leadership and prominent members of influence and respect.

Nations, like individuals, thrive according to material, physical, mental and spiritual qualities. Values of modesty, humility, generosity, tolerance, patience and other virtues are indispensable. The central pursuits of arrogance, corruption, frivolous pleasure and luxury signal a pending demise. The affliction that befalls a nation is often due to the wrong actions of a section of that society, resulting in the disintegration of the whole.

Allah encourages us to travel across the earth and reflect upon great civilizations and people who have disintegrated and vanished. The Qur'an relates situations and events that illustrate examples of people seeking knowledge of the Divine Will, following a spiritual path, who are graced with goodness and growth. The prophet Solomon and his people are such an example. Due to his knowledge, sincere and total submission, and perfection of his worship, Solomon had access to the powers of the invisible realm as well as other supernatural powers. He had dispensation of both the outward and the inward.

In the same way that individuals grow, develop and experience successes and failures and subsequently weaken, decline and die, nations too follow the same type of pattern. A society or a nation is as strong as the quality of its individual members and their leadership.

If a society is lead by wise, just and illumined leaders who have responsible attitudes toward God and the hereafter, and who apply real justice while caring for the weak, it will naturally be a superior culture.

1.

ٱلْحَاقَّةُ ۝ مَا ٱلْحَاقَّةُ ۝ وَمَا أَدْرَىٰكَ مَا ٱلْحَاقَّةُ ۝ كَذَّبَتْ ثَمُودُ وَعَادٌۢ بِٱلْقَارِعَةِ ۝ فَأَمَّا ثَمُودُ فَأُهْلِكُوا۟ بِٱلطَّاغِيَةِ ۝ وَأَمَّا عَادٌ فَأُهْلِكُوا۟ بِرِيحٍ صَرْصَرٍ عَاتِيَةٍ ۝ سَخَّرَهَا عَلَيْهِمْ سَبْعَ لَيَالٍ وَثَمَـٰنِيَةَ أَيَّامٍ حُسُومًا فَتَرَى ٱلْقَوْمَ فِيهَا صَرْعَىٰ كَأَنَّهُمْ أَعْجَازُ نَخْلٍ خَاوِيَةٍ ۝

The Inevitable! What is the Inevitable? What will convey to you what the Inevitable is? Thamud and 'Ad denied the crushing blow. Thamud were destroyed by the deafening blast. 'Ad were destroyed by the savage howling wind. Allah subjected them to it for seven nights and eight days without a break. You could see the people flattened in their homes just like the hollow stumps of uprooted palms. Do you see any remnants of them left?

69/1-8

2.

وَجَآءَ فِرْعَوْنُ وَمَن قَبْلَهُۥ وَٱلْمُؤْتَفِكَـٰتُ بِٱلْخَاطِئَةِ ۝ فَعَصَوْا۟ رَسُولَ رَبِّهِمْ فَأَخَذَهُمْ أَخْذَةً رَّابِيَةً ۝ إِنَّا لَمَّا طَغَا ٱلْمَآءُ حَمَلْنَـٰكُمْ فِى ٱلْجَارِيَةِ ۝ لِنَجْعَلَهَا لَكُمْ تَذْكِرَةً وَتَعِيَهَآ أُذُنٌ وَٰعِيَةٌ ۝ فَإِذَا نُفِخَ فِى ٱلصُّورِ نَفْخَةٌ وَٰحِدَةٌ ۝ وَحُمِلَتِ ٱلْأَرْضُ وَٱلْجِبَالُ فَدُكَّتَا دَكَّةً وَٰحِدَةً ۝ فَيَوْمَئِذٍ وَقَعَتِ ٱلْوَاقِعَةُ ۝

Pharaoh and those before him and the overturned cities made a great mistake. They disobeyed the Messenger of their Lord, so He seized them in an ever-tightening grip. Indeed, when the waters rose, We carried you in the ship, So that it may be a reminder for you and to be retained by retentive ears. When the Trumpet is blown with a single blast, and the earth and the mountains are lifted and crushed with a single blow, on that day shall the Great Event come to pass.

69/9-15

The challenge to all human beings is the discovery and the knowledge of the Divine Creator. This unveiling comes through submission to his ways and laws. Unless intention and conduct lead to enlightenment, the end result is failure and regret. We are designed to know, adore and worship the One.

In every land and within all cultures we can see examples of success and failure due to either excessive worldliness or spiritual yearning and progress. There is no doubt that every created entity will perish at some time or another and this truth brings about the urgency for spiritual knowledge and enlightenment.

The best of people are those following the prophet and the natural code of conduct with sincerity, faith and selfless actions.

The intention behind creation is to know the Creator and His perfections. Thus, our journey through existence should be with wisdom, illumination and following those who traveled before us on this path.

Due to past habits, love of the ego or self, and the darkness of hearts, people do not heed the prophetic warnings and make excuses to avoid discipline and sacrifice on the path, and the light of the intellect.

His mercy and clemency is so great that individuals and societies are given many opportunities to correct their conduct, awaken to the truth, and recognize the urgency of submission with absorbed awareness and adoration.

3.

كُنتُمْ خَيْرَ أُمَّةٍ أُخْرِجَتْ لِلنَّاسِ تَأْمُرُونَ بِالْمَعْرُوفِ وَتَنْهَوْنَ عَنِ الْمُنكَرِ وَتُؤْمِنُونَ بِاللَّهِ وَلَوْ آمَنَ أَهْلُ الْكِتَابِ لَكَانَ خَيْرًا لَّهُم مِّنْهُمُ الْمُؤْمِنُونَ وَأَكْثَرُهُمُ الْفَاسِقُونَ

You are the best community ever to come forth among mankind. You enjoin right, forbid wrong and have faith in Allah. If the people of the Book were to have faith, it would be better for them. Some of them are believers, but most of them stray from the right course.

3/110

4.

قَدْ خَلَتْ مِن قَبْلِكُمْ سُنَنٌ فَسِيرُوا فِي الْأَرْضِ فَانظُرُوا كَيْفَ كَانَ عَاقِبَةُ الْمُكَذِّبِينَ

Many cultures have passed away before you. So, travel through the earth, and see what the end was of those who disbelieved.

3/137

5.

وَكَمْ أَهْلَكْنَا قَبْلَهُم مِّن قَرْنٍ هُمْ أَشَدُّ مِنْهُم بَطْشًا فَنَقَّبُوا فِي الْبِلَادِ هَلْ مِن مَّحِيصٍ

How many generations before them did We destroy who had greater prowess and traveled through the lands! Did they find any way of escape?

50/36

6.

وَكَذَٰلِكَ مَا أَرْسَلْنَا مِن قَبْلِكَ فِي قَرْيَةٍ مِّن نَّذِيرٍ إِلَّا قَالَ مُتْرَفُوهَا إِنَّا وَجَدْنَا آبَاءَنَا عَلَىٰ أُمَّةٍ وَإِنَّا عَلَىٰ آثَارِهِم مُّقْتَدُونَ

We never sent any warner before you to any city without the affluent among them saying: We found our fathers following a way, and we are simply following in their footsteps.

43/23

7.

وَلَوْ يُؤَاخِذُ اللَّهُ النَّاسَ بِظُلْمِهِم مَّا تَرَكَ عَلَيْهَا مِن دَابَّةٍ وَلَٰكِن يُؤَخِّرُهُمْ إِلَىٰ أَجَلٍ مُّسَمًّى ۖ فَإِذَا جَاءَ أَجَلُهُمْ لَا يَسْتَأْخِرُونَ سَاعَةً ۖ وَلَا يَسْتَقْدِمُونَ

If Allah were to take people to task for their wrong actions, not a single creature would be left (on the earth), but He defers it till a predetermined time. When their specified time arrives, they cannot delay it for a single hour, nor can they bring it forward.

16/61

8.

قُلْ يَا أَيُّهَا الَّذِينَ هَادُوا إِن زَعَمْتُمْ أَنَّكُمْ أَوْلِيَاءُ لِلَّهِ مِن دُونِ النَّاسِ فَتَمَنَّوُا الْمَوْتَ إِن كُنتُمْ صَادِقِينَ وَلَا يَتَمَنَّوْنَهُ أَبَدًا بِمَا قَدَّمَتْ أَيْدِيهِمْ ۚ وَاللَّهُ عَلِيمٌ بِالظَّالِمِينَ

Say: O You who are Jews, if you claim to be the friends of Allah to the exclusion of all other people, then long for death if you are telling the truth. But they will never ever wish for it because of what they have done. Allah knows well the wrongdoers.

62/6-7

9.

وَمَا كَانَ رَبُّكَ لِيُهْلِكَ الْقُرَىٰ بِظُلْمٍ وَأَهْلُهَا مُصْلِحُونَ

Your Lord would never have wrongfully destroyed the cities as long as their inhabitants were putting things right.

11/117

10.

وَقَالَ الرَّسُولُ يَا رَبِّ إِنَّ قَوْمِي اتَّخَذُوا هَٰذَا الْقُرْآنَ مَهْجُورًا

The Messenger said: My Lord, my people treat this Qur'an as something to be ignored.

25/30

Remembrance of death is a great tonic and drive to His Light and inner awakening. Readiness for death and departure from this world will place worldly experiences in perspective and change priorities and concerns.

Allah's ways, His laws and His will were revealed to numerous prophets and messengers as divine 'books'. His primal original source code is made accessible through His messengers. No culture or society is deprived from His 'pen' and the book of Truth. Yet we find His maps and 'books' are neglected or followed only superficially and 'formally'.

Allah's mercy is such that for every people there arose messengers from among themselves like beacons of light, upon the path of submission and appropriate conduct to the eternal truth.

11.

تِلْكَ أُمَّةٌ قَدْ خَلَتْ ۖ لَهَا مَا كَسَبَتْ وَلَكُم مَّا كَسَبْتُمْ ۖ وَلَا تُسْأَلُونَ عَمَّا كَانُوا يَعْمَلُونَ

Nations have passed away, and each has what it earned. You as well have what you earn, and you will not be questioned about what they did.

2/134

12.

وَمَا أَهْلَكْنَا مِن قَرْيَةٍ إِلَّا لَهَا مُنذِرُونَ ذِكْرَىٰ وَمَا كُنَّا ظَالِمِينَ

We have never destroyed a city without giving it prior warning as a reminder, and we have never been unjust.

26/208-209

13.

وَإِن جَادَلُوكَ فَقُلِ اللَّهُ أَعْلَمُ بِمَا تَعْمَلُونَ اللَّهُ يَحْكُمُ بَيْنَكُمْ يَوْمَ الْقِيَامَةِ فِيمَا كُنتُمْ فِيهِ تَخْتَلِفُونَ

On the last Day of Judgment, all beings and people will come to realize what they have missed. In that zone of consciousness, there is nothing one can do to remove the suffocating worldly veils of ignorance and distractions.

We have appointed for every nation a rite that they observe, so let them not dispute with you about the matter. Call the people to your Lord, for assuredly you are rightly guided, and if they argue with you, say: Allah knows best what you are doing. Allah will judge between you on the Day of Rising regarding your differences.

22/67-69

14.

وَٱللَّهُ فَضَّلَ بَعْضَكُمْ عَلَىٰ بَعْضٍ فِى ٱلرِّزْقِ فَمَا ٱلَّذِينَ فُضِّلُوا۟ بِرَآدِّى رِزْقِهِمْ عَلَىٰ مَا مَلَكَتْ أَيْمَٰنُهُمْ فَهُمْ فِيهِ سَوَآءٌ أَفَبِنِعْمَةِ ٱللَّهِ يَجْحَدُونَ

Allah has favoured some of you over others in provision, but those who have been favoured will not give their provisions to their slaves so they become equal. So why do they deny the blessing of Allah?

16/71

In this life there will always be differences in people's health, wealth, and knowledge. Outward differences cloak the innate sameness in the potential for awakening.

15.

لَقَدْ أَنزَلْنَآ إِلَيْكُمْ كِتَٰبًا فِيهِ ذِكْرُكُمْ أَفَلَا تَعْقِلُونَ
وَكَمْ قَصَمْنَا مِن قَرْيَةٍ كَانَتْ ظَالِمَةً وَأَنشَأْنَا بَعْدَهَا قَوْمًا ءَاخَرِينَ
فَلَمَّآ أَحَسُّوا۟ بَأْسَنَآ إِذَا هُم مِّنْهَا يَرْكُضُونَ

We have sent down the Book containing your reminder. So will you not use your intellect? How many cities, which did wrong, have We utterly destroyed, raising up other people after them? When they perceived Our force they took flight from it.

21/10-12

Essentially all of creation has perfection and divine attributes encoded within each individual, and that essential core is seeking to manifest itself. This brilliant light is masked by the shadowy lens of the lower self. Allah's mercy is such that for everyone there are many opportunities for forgiveness and redirection to the eternal truth.

The self is misguided by the constant desire and search for ease and expansion while denying the blessings of constriction and limitation. The latter drives us towards higher meanings and perfections through humility and self-effacement, sensitivity, reliance and awareness of the One essence.

In this world of material and physical dominance, the most greedy and unjust people often end up as rulers.

Natural disasters and social afflictions come about as a result of misconduct and arrogance of individuals as well as in societies.

16.

وَإِذَا مَسَّ ٱلنَّاسَ ضُرٌّ دَعَوْا رَبَّهُم مُّنِيبِينَ إِلَيْهِ ثُمَّ إِذَآ أَذَاقَهُم مِّنْهُ رَحْمَةً إِذَا فَرِيقٌ مِّنْهُم بِرَبِّهِمْ يُشْرِكُونَ

When harm touches people, they call upon their Lord, turning to Him in repentance; then, when He causes them to taste of His mercy, a group of them immediately associate others with their Lord.

30/33

17.

وَلَوْ بَسَطَ ٱللَّهُ ٱلرِّزْقَ لِعِبَادِهِۦ لَبَغَوْا فِى ٱلْأَرْضِ وَلَٰكِن يُنَزِّلُ بِقَدَرٍ مَّا يَشَآءُ إِنَّهُۥ بِعِبَادِهِۦ خَبِيرٌۢ بَصِيرٌ

Were Allah to expand His provisions for His slaves, they would covet and oppress, so He sends down whatever He wills in a measured way. He is aware of and sees His slaves.

42/27

18.

وَكَذَٰلِكَ جَعَلْنَا فِى كُلِّ قَرْيَةٍ أَكَابِرَ مُجْرِمِيهَا لِيَمْكُرُوا فِيهَا وَمَا يَمْكُرُونَ إِلَّا بِأَنفُسِهِمْ وَمَا يَشْعُرُونَ

In every city We place great wrongdoers to deceive, delude and cheat. In reality, they only do these things to themselves, but they are completely unaware.

6/123

19.

وَإِذَآ أَرَدْنَآ أَن نُّهْلِكَ قَرْيَةً أَمَرْنَا مُتْرَفِيهَا فَفَسَقُوا فِيهَا فَحَقَّ عَلَيْهَا ٱلْقَوْلُ فَدَمَّرْنَٰهَا تَدْمِيرًا

When We desire to destroy a city, We inform its affluent, who are immoral and iniquitous. Then the Word is justly carried out against it, and We destroy it completely.

17/16

20.

قَالَتْ إِنَّ الْمُلُوكَ إِذَا دَخَلُوا قَرْيَةً أَفْسَدُوهَا وَجَعَلُوا أَعِزَّةَ أَهْلِهَا أَذِلَّةً وَكَذَٰلِكَ يَفْعَلُونَ

She (Bilkis) said: when kings enter a city, they ruin it and make the mightiest and noblest of its inhabitants the most abased. That is what they too will do.

27/34

Human hypocrisy is given legitimacy by the lower tendencies of the self. It is a dreadful veil of self-deception. Thus justification is given by despotic kings and power-seeking rulers.

21.

الْمُنَافِقُونَ وَالْمُنَافِقَاتُ بَعْضُهُم مِّن بَعْضٍ يَأْمُرُونَ بِالْمُنكَرِ وَيَنْهَوْنَ عَنِ الْمَعْرُوفِ وَيَقْبِضُونَ أَيْدِيَهُمْ نَسُوا اللَّهَ فَنَسِيَهُمْ إِنَّ الْمُنَافِقِينَ هُمُ الْفَاسِقُونَ

The hypocrites, both men and women, are all alike. They enjoin wrong, forbid right, and keep their hands tightly closed. They have forgotten Allah, so He has forgotten them. The hypocrites stray from the right course.

9/67

The hypocrites strengthen each other in their forgetfulness and darkness in this transient world.

22.

مِنْ أَجْلِ ذَٰلِكَ كَتَبْنَا عَلَىٰ بَنِي إِسْرَائِيلَ أَنَّهُ مَن قَتَلَ نَفْسًا بِغَيْرِ نَفْسٍ أَوْ فَسَادٍ فِي الْأَرْضِ فَكَأَنَّمَا قَتَلَ النَّاسَ جَمِيعًا وَمَنْ أَحْيَاهَا فَكَأَنَّمَا أَحْيَا النَّاسَ جَمِيعًا وَلَقَدْ جَاءَتْهُمْ رُسُلُنَا بِالْبَيِّنَاتِ ثُمَّ إِنَّ كَثِيرًا مِّنْهُم بَعْدَ ذَٰلِكَ فِي الْأَرْضِ لَمُسْرِفُونَ

We decreed for the tribe of Israel that if someone kills another person – unless it is in retaliation for someone else or for causing corruption in the earth – it is as if he had murdered all mankind. And one who gives life; it is as if he has given life to all of mankind. Certainly our messengers came with clear signs, but even after that many of them continued to live immoderately.

5/32

The Adamic self emanates from one universal design. Thus if one being is enlightened all of humanity will benefit.

The Adamic offspring are like one global tribe. What affects a few members will affect the rest. We are all responsible and cannot ignore evil acts, even if they do not have immediate or obvious adverse consequences. Every action will have its effect, but often it is not measurable or immediately discernible.

23.

وَاتَّقُوا فِتْنَةً لَّا تُصِيبَنَّ الَّذِينَ ظَلَمُوا مِنكُمْ خَاصَّةً وَاعْلَمُوا أَنَّ اللَّهَ شَدِيدُ الْعِقَابِ

Be extremely cautious of trials that will not only afflict those among you who do wrong. Know that Allah is firm in consequence.

8/25

24.

وَجَعَلْنَا ابْنَ مَرْيَمَ وَأُمَّهُ آيَةً وَآوَيْنَاهُمَا إِلَىٰ رَبْوَةٍ ذَاتِ قَرَارٍ وَمَعِينٍ
يَا أَيُّهَا الرُّسُلُ كُلُوا مِنَ الطَّيِّبَاتِ وَاعْمَلُوا صَالِحًا إِنِّي بِمَا تَعْمَلُونَ عَلِيمٌ
وَإِنَّ هَٰذِهِ أُمَّتُكُمْ أُمَّةً وَاحِدَةً وَأَنَا رَبُّكُمْ فَاتَّقُونِ
فَتَقَطَّعُوا أَمْرَهُم بَيْنَهُمْ زُبُرًا كُلُّ حِزْبٍ بِمَا لَدَيْهِمْ فَرِحُونَ
فَذَرْهُمْ فِي غَمْرَتِهِمْ حَتَّىٰ حِينٍ
أَيَحْسَبُونَ أَنَّمَا نُمِدُّهُم بِهِ مِن مَّالٍ وَبَنِينَ
نُسَارِعُ لَهُمْ فِي الْخَيْرَاتِ بَل لَّا يَشْعُرُونَ

All human beings are under the sovereignty of the Lord and all His true messengers who had traveled the same path in different times. Yet cultural differences and societal factions occur due to lack of knowledge of the ultimate divine purpose. Jesus and his mother were great signs and gifts to mankind yet for worldly considerations we lose sight of the inner message.

And we made the son of Mary and his mother a sign, and We gave them shelter on a lofty ground where there was a resting place and a flowing spring. O Messengers, eat of the good things and act righteously. Surely I know what you do. Indeed this community is a single community and I am your Lord, so be cautiously aware of Me. But they disagreed and split up, dividing into sects, each party exulting in what they had. So leave them in their overwhelming ignorance. Do they imagine that in the wealth and children We extend to them, We hasten to them good things? Indeed, but they have no perception!

23/50-56

25.

$$\text{وَلَوْ أَنَّ أَهْلَ الْقُرَىٰ آمَنُوا وَاتَّقَوْا لَفَتَحْنَا عَلَيْهِم بَرَكَاتٍ مِّنَ السَّمَاءِ وَالْأَرْضِ وَلَٰكِن كَذَّبُوا فَأَخَذْنَاهُم بِمَا كَانُوا يَكْسِبُونَ}$$

If only the people of the cities had believed and had cautious awareness, We would have opened up for them blessings from the heavens and earth. But they denied the truth, so We overtook them for what they earned.

7/96

26.

$$\text{قُلْ أَعُوذُ بِرَبِّ النَّاسِ}$$
$$\text{مَلِكِ النَّاسِ}$$
$$\text{إِلَٰهِ النَّاسِ}$$
$$\text{مِن شَرِّ الْوَسْوَاسِ الْخَنَّاسِ}$$
$$\text{الَّذِي يُوَسْوِسُ فِي صُدُورِ النَّاسِ}$$
$$\text{مِنَ الْجِنَّةِ وَالنَّاسِ}$$

Say: I seek refuge with the Lord of mankind, the King of mankind, the God of mankind, from the evil of the insidious whisperer who whispers in the hearts of mankind, and comes from among the invisible entities and from mankind.

If a person or society truly lives in the light of faith and reliance on Him, then all the bounties from heaven and earth would be experienced. The ignorant human self is the barrier for this realization.

The Creator of mankind has given the option of evil acts and good ones. Thus we seek His protection and guidance from all the destructive energies both within us and outside of us, known and unknown. We need to refer to Him at all times. It is our duty to constantly call upon His mercy and forgiveness.

CHAPTER ELEVEN

BELIEVERS

The purpose of the path is to enable those who have faith in Allah to witness His unique oneness and know His presence in every situation at all times. The believer (*mu'min*) lives the Qur'anic way and adopts the prophetic qualities and actions. He is sincere, trustworthy, wise, moderate, generous, forgiving, selfless, friendly, reliable, does not oppress, aids the needy, earns a legitimate livelihood, acts with forbearance when facing adversity, enduring hardships with fortitude. The believer strives at all times to understand the reason and meaning behind events and corrects his wrong actions as soon as he becomes aware of his shortcomings. He will act in good faith, rationally, and with good counsel in matters to do with the world whilst constantly realizing his accountability to Allah the Ever-Forgiving, Merciful Guide.

The believer does his utmost without expectations of anyone other than Allah who is always in charge. A believer starts his journey with the faith that his ignorance will be replaced with knowledge and his confusion with certainty. As one progresses in life, this initial faith in Divine Grace will translate into knowledge of the Divine Presence. This higher awareness brings about sensitivity, accountability and a sense of heightened inspiration that improves his intention and direction at all times. The believer is journeying to Allah, by Allah's guidance and under His protection. Thus the lovers of Allah experience no grief nor do they lack in courage or great expectations from their Creator the All-Generous and Most Merciful.

The sincere and responsible seeker of truth will read, study and reflect upon the verses (*āyāt*) of the Qur'an and apply their meaning and boundaries. The true believer knows that all of existence is subject to the decrees and laws of a most glorious Creator. Thus he is always content at heart whilst striving outwardly and inwardly with service and goodness dedicated to the source of all goodness.

1.

قَدْ أَفْلَحَ ٱلْمُؤْمِنُونَ ۝ ٱلَّذِينَ هُمْ فِي صَلَاتِهِمْ خَاشِعُونَ ۝ وَٱلَّذِينَ هُمْ عَنِ ٱللَّغْوِ مُعْرِضُونَ ۝ وَٱلَّذِينَ هُمْ لِلزَّكَوٰةِ فَاعِلُونَ ۝ وَٱلَّذِينَ هُمْ لِفُرُوجِهِمْ حَافِظُونَ ۝ إِلَّا عَلَىٰٓ أَزْوَاجِهِمْ أَوْ مَا مَلَكَتْ أَيْمَانُهُمْ فَإِنَّهُمْ غَيْرُ مَلُومِينَ ۝ فَمَنِ ٱبْتَغَىٰ وَرَآءَ ذَٰلِكَ فَأُو۟لَٰٓئِكَ هُمُ ٱلْعَادُونَ ۝ وَٱلَّذِينَ هُمْ لِأَمَانَاتِهِمْ وَعَهْدِهِمْ رَاعُونَ ۝ وَٱلَّذِينَ هُمْ عَلَىٰ صَلَوَاتِهِمْ يُحَافِظُونَ ۝ أُو۟لَٰٓئِكَ هُمُ ٱلْوَارِثُونَ ۝ ٱلَّذِينَ يَرِثُونَ ٱلْفِرْدَوْسَ هُمْ فِيهَا خَالِدُونَ ۝

Successful indeed are the believers who are humble in their prayer, and who turn away from useless conversation; those who pay alms tax for the poor and guard their modesty, except with their wives or their slaves, in which case they are not blameworthy. But those who desire anything more than that are people who have gone beyond the limits. And those who honour their trust and contracts, and safeguard their prayer, are the inheritors, who will inherit Paradise, remaining in it forever, beyond time.

23/1-11

This life is only a prelude to another phase of being where the experience is lasting. This insight regarding the hereafter is the foundation of faith.

The price of paradise is total surrender to the highest within us whilst controlling the lower tendencies with constant vigilance and alertness.

2.

إِنَّمَا ٱلْمُؤْمِنُونَ ٱلَّذِينَ إِذَا ذُكِرَ ٱللَّهُ وَجِلَتْ قُلُوبُهُمْ وَإِذَا تُلِيَتْ عَلَيْهِمْ آيَاتُهُ زَادَتْهُمْ إِيمَانًا وَعَلَىٰ رَبِّهِمْ يَتَوَكَّلُونَ

The believers are those whose hearts tremble when Allah is mentioned, whose faith is increased when His signs are recited to them, and who put their trust completely in their Lord

8/2

3.

يَٰٓأَيُّهَا ٱلَّذِينَ آمَنُوا۟ ٱتَّقُوا۟ ٱللَّهَ وَٱبْتَغُوٓا۟ إِلَيْهِ ٱلْوَسِيلَةَ وَجَٰهِدُوا۟ فِي سَبِيلِهِ لَعَلَّكُمْ تُفْلِحُونَ

O You who believe, be cautiously aware of Allah, and seek the means of access to Him, and strive in His way, so that hopefully you will be successful.

5/35

Disciplined effort towards the higher whilst maintaining a pure heart is the ingredient for lasting success. To expect the least from creation and the best from the Creator is the order for the wayfarer. Whoever serves the Creator will find creation serving him.

All success comes by following His decrees and unifying our will with His.

4.

إِن يَنصُرْكُمُ اللَّهُ فَلَا غَالِبَ لَكُمْ ۖ وَإِن يَخْذُلْكُمْ فَمَن ذَا الَّذِي يَنصُرُكُم مِّن بَعْدِهِ ۗ وَعَلَى اللَّهِ فَلْيَتَوَكَّلِ الْمُؤْمِنُونَ

If Allah assists you none can overcome you, and if He withdraws His help from you, who is there who can help you besides Him? Upon Allah let the believers depend

3/160

5.

وَالَّذِينَ آمَنُوا وَهَاجَرُوا وَجَاهَدُوا فِي سَبِيلِ اللَّهِ وَالَّذِينَ آوَوا وَّنَصَرُوا أُولَٰئِكَ هُمُ الْمُؤْمِنُونَ حَقًّا ۚ لَّهُم مَّغْفِرَةٌ وَرِزْقٌ كَرِيمٌ

Those who have faith and have migrated and have striven in the way of Allah, and those who have given refuge and help, they are the true believers. They will have forgiveness and a generous provision.

8/74

The whole universe is in need at all times. To awaken to this truth will set the seeker free of illusions of independence from Him or reliance on 'other than Allah'. If one's priority is to obey Him, the rest will follow with ease and in perfect order.

6.

سَيَهْدِيهِمْ وَيُصْلِحُ بَالَهُمْ وَيُدْخِلُهُمُ الْجَنَّةَ عَرَّفَهَا لَهُمْ يَا أَيُّهَا الَّذِينَ آمَنُوا إِن تَنصُرُوا اللَّهَ يَنصُرْكُمْ وَيُثَبِّتْ أَقْدَامَكُمْ

He will guide them and improve their condition; And He will admit them into the Garden, which He has made known to them. O you who believe, if you help Allah, He will help you and make your feet firm.

47/5-7

Human beings always seek physical, mental and spiritual provision. These pursuits are in order to realize the One provider, the nurturer and the ever-loving Creator of the ever-lasting human soul.

7.

وَمَن يَتَّقِ اللَّهَ يَجْعَل لَّهُ مَخْرَجًا وَيَرْزُقْهُ مِنْ حَيْثُ لَا يَحْتَسِبُ ۚ وَمَن يَتَوَكَّلْ عَلَى اللَّهِ فَهُوَ حَسْبُهُ ۚ إِنَّ اللَّهَ بَالِغُ أَمْرِهِ ۚ قَدْ جَعَلَ اللَّهُ لِكُلِّ شَيْءٍ قَدْرًا

…And whoever has cautious awareness of Allah, He will open a way, and provide for him from where he does not expect. Whoever puts his trust in Allah, He will be enough for him. Allah always achieves His aim. Indeed, Allah has appointed a measure for all things.

65/2-3

8.

$$\text{الَّذِينَ آمَنُوا وَتَطْمَئِنُّ قُلُوبُهُم بِذِكْرِ اللَّهِ أَلَا بِذِكْرِ اللَّهِ تَطْمَئِنُّ الْقُلُوبُ}$$

Those who believe and whose hearts find serenity in the remembrance of Allah. Only in the remembrance of Allah can the heart find peace.

13/28

9.

$$\text{إِنَّ الَّذِينَ آمَنُوا وَعَمِلُوا الصَّالِحَاتِ وَأَخْبَتُوا إِلَىٰ رَبِّهِمْ أُولَٰئِكَ أَصْحَابُ الْجَنَّةِ هُمْ فِيهَا خَالِدُونَ}$$

Truly, those who believe and act righteously, humbling themselves before their Lord, are the companions of the Garden, remaining in it beyond time.

11/23

10.

$$\text{وَالَّذِينَ لَا يَشْهَدُونَ الزُّورَ وَإِذَا مَرُّوا بِاللَّغْوِ مَرُّوا كِرَامًا}$$

Those who do not acknowledge what is false, and when they encounter senseless talk leave it and maintain their dignity.

25/72

11.

$$\text{وَالَّذِينَ هُمْ لِأَمَانَاتِهِمْ وَعَهْدِهِمْ رَاعُونَ وَالَّذِينَ هُم بِشَهَادَاتِهِمْ قَائِمُونَ وَالَّذِينَ هُمْ عَلَىٰ صَلَاتِهِمْ يُحَافِظُونَ أُولَٰئِكَ فِي جَنَّاتٍ مُّكْرَمُونَ}$$

Those who honour their promises and contracts; Who are upright in their testimony; Who are attentive in their worship - These are in Paradise, highly honoured.

70/32-35

Human memory is a most useful faculty as well as a barrier. Its origin is in the world of the unseen rooted in the divine light. Only by remembering Him (the oldest memory) do our hearts become content and tranquil.

The vigilant believer respects all of creation because it all belongs to the One Creator. Care for living is a reflection of the One who is ever living.

Whoever combines the virtues of courage, modesty, wisdom and justice is well groomed and disciplined in good ethics. These four key qualities are the spiritual foundation of the illumined 'Ka'bah' in the heart.

12.

صِبْغَةَ اللَّهِ وَمَنْ أَحْسَنُ مِنَ اللَّهِ صِبْغَةً وَنَحْنُ لَهُ عَابِدُونَ

The colouring is Allah's – who is better in colouring than Allah? We worship Him alone.

2/138

Enlightened beings are cloaked by many of the divine qualities and attributes such as mercy, generosity, patience, knowledge, etc. These are Allah's attributes or colours, which He bestows upon His humble and true servants. Those who are wise by their self-effacement and love of His perfections.

13

الَّذِينَ قَالَ لَهُمُ النَّاسُ إِنَّ النَّاسَ قَدْ جَمَعُوا لَكُمْ فَاخْشَوْهُمْ فَزَادَهُمْ إِيمَانًا وَقَالُوا حَسْبُنَا اللَّهُ وَنِعْمَ الْوَكِيلُ
فَانْقَلَبُوا بِنِعْمَةٍ مِنَ اللَّهِ وَفَضْلٍ لَمْ يَمْسَسْهُمْ سُوءٌ وَاتَّبَعُوا رِضْوَانَ اللَّهِ وَاللَّهُ ذُو فَضْلٍ عَظِيمٍ
إِنَّمَا ذَٰلِكُمُ الشَّيْطَانُ يُخَوِّفُ أَوْلِيَاءَهُ فَلَا تَخَافُوهُمْ وَخَافُونِ إِنْ كُنْتُمْ مُؤْمِنِينَ

Those to whom people said: A group has gathered against you, so fear them. But that merely increased their faith, and they said: Allah is enough for us and is the best of Guardians. So they returned with favour and bounty from Allah, and no harm touched them. They followed the pleasure of Allah and Allah possesses infinite bounty. Iblīs only frightens through his partisans. Do not fear them – fear Me if you are believers.

3/173-175

Real strength comes from remembrance and reliance upon Allah in all situations.

14.

رَبَّنَا لَا تَجْعَلْنَا فِتْنَةً لِلَّذِينَ كَفَرُوا وَاغْفِرْ لَنَا رَبَّنَا إِنَّكَ أَنْتَ الْعَزِيزُ الْحَكِيمُ

Our Lord, do not make us a target for those who disbelieve and forgive us. Indeed, You are the Almighty, the All-wise.

60/5

Only Allah brings about real freedom from other than Him. Focusing on the root of a tree, the movement of branches will have little disturbing effect.

15.

وَلَوْلَا فَضْلُ اللَّهِ عَلَيْكُمْ وَرَحْمَتُهُ وَأَنَّ اللَّهَ رَءُوفٌ رَّحِيمٌ

Were it not for Allah's favour to you and His mercy, and that Allah is compassionate, most Merciful.

24/20

16.

يَا أَيُّهَا النَّبِيُّ قُل لِّمَن فِي أَيْدِيكُم مِّنَ الْأَسْرَىٰ إِن يَعْلَمِ اللَّهُ فِي قُلُوبِكُمْ خَيْرًا يُؤْتِكُمْ خَيْرًا مِّمَّا أُخِذَ مِنكُمْ وَيَغْفِرْ لَكُمْ ۗ وَاللَّهُ غَفُورٌ رَّحِيمٌ

O Prophet, Say to those you are holding prisoner: If Allah knows of any good in your hearts, He will give you something better than what has been taken away from you, and He will forgive you. Allah is Ever-Forgiving, Most Merciful.

8/70

17.

وَمَن يَتَّقِ اللَّهَ يَجْعَل لَّهُ مِنْ أَمْرِهِ يُسْرًا

Whoever has full awareness of Allah, He will make matters easy for him.

65/4

18.

وَلِيَعْلَمَ الَّذِينَ أُوتُوا الْعِلْمَ أَنَّهُ الْحَقُّ مِن رَّبِّكَ فَيُؤْمِنُوا بِهِ فَتُخْبِتَ لَهُ قُلُوبُهُمْ ۗ وَإِنَّ اللَّهَ لَهَادِ الَّذِينَ آمَنُوا إِلَىٰ صِرَاطٍ مُّسْتَقِيمٍ

Those who have been given knowledge will certainly know that it is the truth from their Lord, and they will believe in it, and their hearts will be humbled to Him. Allah guides those who believe to a straight path.

22/54

There will always be troubles and turmoil in this world. To look for the original cause, which is the meaning and reason behind the events, could lead to a better future wisdom. Our intellect desires freedom from the changing dramas and tragedies. We seek durable equilibrium and balance in life. This is the spiritual quest and consciousness

The safety of the wayfarer is based on fearful awareness of Allah's might and power as well as His mercy, generosity and forgiveness.

Joyful events in this world are a small sample of what is to be expected in the Hereafter. This world is a trial run for the next, and human beings in this world are practicing for the tranquil garden or the fiery turmoil of the next world. Samples of paradise and hell abound here, in this life.

When a seeker is overwhelmed by difficulties, which are hindrances to our spiritual progress, Allah commands migration to other abodes.

The intelligent seeker takes constant refuge in inner tranquility and contentment. The believer grows in spiritual wisdom and avoids most of the worldly temptation.

The outer world is but distraction and veiling from the perfect Light and Source within. The human self is the veil to witnessing Him, yet without it there would be no life and growth on earth.

19.

يَا عِبَادِيَ الَّذِينَ آمَنُوا إِنَّ أَرْضِي وَاسِعَةٌ فَإِيَّايَ فَاعْبُدُونِ

O My slaves who believe, My earth is wide, so worship Me alone.

29/56

20.

يَا قَوْمِ إِنَّمَا هَذِهِ الْحَيَاةُ الدُّنْيَا مَتَاعٌ وَإِنَّ الْآخِرَةَ هِيَ دَارُ الْقَرَارِ

The man who believed said: my people follow me, and I will show you the path of guidance. O My people, the life of the world is but an enjoyment, but the Hereafter is most certainly the abode of permanence.

40/39

21.

الَّذِينَ يَتَرَبَّصُونَ بِكُمْ فَإِنْ كَانَ لَكُمْ فَتْحٌ مِنَ اللَّهِ قَالُوا أَلَمْ نَكُنْ مَعَكُمْ وَإِنْ كَانَ لِلْكَافِرِينَ نَصِيبٌ قَالُوا أَلَمْ نَسْتَحْوِذْ عَلَيْكُمْ وَنَمْنَعْكُمْ مِنَ الْمُؤْمِنِينَ فَاللَّهُ يَحْكُمُ بَيْنَكُمْ يَوْمَ الْقِيَامَةِ وَلَنْ يَجْعَلَ اللَّهُ لِلْكَافِرِينَ عَلَى الْمُؤْمِنِينَ سَبِيلًا

Whenever you gain a victory from Allah those who waited to see what would happen to you say: Were we not with you? But if the disbelievers have a success they say (to the disbelievers): Did we not have the upper hand over you and keep the believers away from you? Allah will judge between you on the Day of Rising. Allah will not allow the disbelievers any way against the believers

4/141

22.

يَا أَيُّهَا الَّذِينَ آمَنُوا لَا تَتَوَلَّوْا قَوْمًا غَضِبَ اللَّهُ عَلَيْهِمْ قَدْ يَئِسُوا مِنَ الْآخِرَةِ كَمَا يَئِسَ الْكُفَّارُ مِنْ أَصْحَابِ الْقُبُورِ

O You who believe, do not befriend people with whom Allah is angry, who have despaired of the Hereafter as the unbelievers have despaired of the inhabitants of the graves.

60/13

23.

يَـٰٓأَيُّهَا ٱلَّذِينَ ءَامَنُوٓا۟ إِنَّ مِنْ أَزْوَٰجِكُمْ وَأَوْلَـٰدِكُمْ عَدُوًّا لَّكُمْ فَٱحْذَرُوهُمْ وَإِن تَعْفُوا۟ وَتَصْفَحُوا۟ وَتَغْفِرُوا۟ فَإِنَّ ٱللَّهَ غَفُورٌ رَّحِيمٌ

O You who believe, among your wives and children there may be those who oppose you, so be wary of them. But if you pardon, overlook and forgive, Allah is Ever-Forgiving, Most Merciful.

64/14

It is said that paradise is surrounded by hell fire and hell is encircled by gardens. What starts with ease and temptation can end up with great distress and affliction.

25.

أَحَسِبَ ٱلنَّاسُ أَن يُتْرَكُوٓا۟ أَن يَقُولُوٓا۟ ءَامَنَّا وَهُمْ لَا يُفْتَنُونَ
وَلَقَدْ فَتَنَّا ٱلَّذِينَ مِن قَبْلِهِمْ فَلَيَعْلَمَنَّ ٱللَّهُ ٱلَّذِينَ صَدَقُوا۟ وَلَيَعْلَمَنَّ ٱلْكَـٰذِبِينَ

Do people imagine that they will be left to say: We believe, and then they will not be tested? We tested those before them so that Allah would know the sincere and the insincere.

29/2-3

No human being is ever spared from the trials and tribulations of the changing world. What matters is one's attitude, steadfastness, deeper insight and awakening to meanings and messages beyond events. These condition our response to future events.

People's injustice is due to refusal to follow the prescribed divine path, which brings about illumination and return to His glorious presence. The vigilant seeker must resist deviation and injustice wherever and whenever possible.

Rejection of His will is darkness, ignorance and deprivation of the true gift and purpose of life.

The human heart desires, tranquility and peace. Any experience that disturbs the heart's wholesomeness is a distraction that may lead to sickness of the heart and body.

Wrongdoing will eventually cause the perpetrator's downfall and banishment. Thus constant watchfulness and awareness of our intention and action is essential for safe passage and spiritual growth.

26.

وَمِنَ النَّاسِ مَن يَقُولُ آمَنَّا بِاللَّهِ فَإِذَا أُوذِيَ فِي اللَّهِ جَعَلَ فِتْنَةَ النَّاسِ كَعَذَابِ اللَّهِ وَلَئِن جَاءَ نَصْرٌ مِّن رَّبِّكَ لَيَقُولُنَّ إِنَّا كُنَّا مَعَكُمْ أَوَلَيْسَ اللَّهُ بِأَعْلَمَ بِمَا فِي صُدُورِ الْعَالَمِينَ

There are some people who say: We believe in Allah, but when they suffer harm in Allah's way, they take people's persecution for Allah's punishment. When help comes from your Lord they say: We were with you. Is Allah not fully aware of what is in every person's heart?
29/10

27.

إِن تَكْفُرُوا فَإِنَّ اللَّهَ غَنِيٌّ عَنكُمْ وَلَا يَرْضَىٰ لِعِبَادِهِ الْكُفْرَ وَإِن تَشْكُرُوا يَرْضَهُ لَكُمْ وَلَا تَزِرُ وَازِرَةٌ وِزْرَ أُخْرَىٰ ثُمَّ إِلَىٰ رَبِّكُم مَّرْجِعُكُمْ فَيُنَبِّئُكُم بِمَا كُنتُمْ تَعْمَلُونَ إِنَّهُ عَلِيمٌ بِذَاتِ الصُّدُورِ

If you are ungrateful, Allah is rich beyond need of you, and He is not pleased with ingratitude from His slaves. But if you are grateful, He is pleased with you. No one can bear another's burden. To your Lord is the return and He will inform you of what you have done. He knows what the heart contains.
39/7

28.

يَا أَيُّهَا الَّذِينَ آمَنُوا لَا يَسْخَرْ قَوْمٌ مِّن قَوْمٍ عَسَىٰ أَن يَكُونُوا خَيْرًا مِّنْهُمْ وَلَا نِسَاءٌ مِّن نِّسَاءٍ عَسَىٰ أَن يَكُنَّ خَيْرًا مِّنْهُنَّ وَلَا تَلْمِزُوا أَنفُسَكُمْ وَلَا تَنَابَزُوا بِالْأَلْقَابِ بِئْسَ الِاسْمُ الْفُسُوقُ بَعْدَ الْإِيمَانِ وَمَن لَّمْ يَتُبْ فَأُولَٰئِكَ هُمُ الظَّالِمُونَ

O you who believe, people should not ridicule others who may be better than they are; nor should women ridicule other women who may be better than they are. And do not find fault with one another or insult each other with derogatory nicknames. It is wrong to call (someone by) a bad name after (having) faith. Whoever does not turn away from these actions are wrongdoers.
49/11

29.

وَاتَّقُوا يَوْمًا تُرْجَعُونَ فِيهِ إِلَى اللَّهِ ۖ ثُمَّ تُوَفَّىٰ كُلُّ نَفْسٍ مَّا كَسَبَتْ وَهُمْ لَا يُظْلَمُونَ

Guard your selves from a Day when you will be returned to Allah. Then every soul will be repaid for what it earned, and they will not be wronged.

2/281

By our actions in this world we are prescribing our state in the hereafter where we shall experience what we have sown here.

CHAPTER TWELVE

UNBELIEVERS

The unbelievers (*kāfirūn*) are those who are encapsulated in darkness and ignorance away from the brilliant, prevailing Divine Light. They are not on the path of spiritual development and arrival to the unique Source of existence and creation. They are preoccupied with the ever-changing causality of this world and the pursuit of material and physical things and common pleasures.

The unbeliever does not realize that this life is a prelude to the Hereafter and that all actions and thoughts in this world will be lived through in the next phase. If a person is not convinced of the ongoingness of life after death, then worldly matters become the primary objective and goal.

The unbelievers have no belief in the One, All-pervading Creator. Therefore, everything in their life is transient and has only worldly significance. They may gain power and wealth in this life, but they will miss the eternal garden in the next. The unbelievers obstruct the natural primal patterns within themselves that are available in order to develop and guide them towards witnessing the One Source and Essence.

The maps and full atlas of the journey in this life are reflected in the practices of Islam. These practices provide a prophetically proven path of travel from the darkness of outer uncertainty to the realm of inner security and light. Whoever is veiled from the desire and drive towards the truth will also be deprived of true surrender or Islam, which is the means of arriving at the truth. If one has no desire or urge to reach the destination, one has no need for a map or safe travel. The unbeliever is veiled from the glorious experiences of being in the Divine Presence.

Unbelievers

1.

قُلْ يَا أَيُّهَا الْكَافِرُونَ
لَا أَعْبُدُ مَا تَعْبُدُونَ
وَلَا أَنتُمْ عَابِدُونَ مَا أَعْبُدُ
وَلَا أَنَا عَابِدٌ مَّا عَبَدتُّمْ
وَلَا أَنتُمْ عَابِدُونَ مَا أَعْبُدُ
لَكُمْ دِينُكُمْ وَلِيَ دِينِ

Say: O Unbelievers, I do not worship what you worship, nor do you worship what I worship, and I will not worship what you worship, nor will you worship what I worship. You have your way, and I have my way (dīn).

109/1-6

2.

إِنَّ الَّذِينَ لَا يُؤْمِنُونَ بِالْآخِرَةِ زَيَّنَّا لَهُمْ أَعْمَالَهُمْ فَهُمْ يَعْمَهُونَ

Indeed, for those who do not believe in the hereafter, We have made their actions attractive to them and they blindly wander on.

27/4

3.

وَالَّذِينَ كَفَرُوا بِآيَاتِ اللَّهِ وَلِقَائِهِ أُولَٰئِكَ يَئِسُوا مِن رَّحْمَتِي وَأُولَٰئِكَ لَهُمْ عَذَابٌ أَلِيمٌ

Those who deny Allah's signs and the meeting with Him despair of My mercy; they will suffer a painful punishment.

29/23

4.

وَلَا تَيْأَسُوا مِن رَّوْحِ اللَّهِ إِنَّهُ لَا يَيْأَسُ مِن رَّوْحِ اللَّهِ إِلَّا الْقَوْمُ الْكَافِرُونَ

Do not despair of Allah's mercy. No one despairs of Allah's mercy except for the people who disbelieve.

12/87

All human beings are seekers of eternal divine light. The unfortunate and ignorant beings are those engulfed in the darkness of the lower self. They are deprived of the spiritual nourishment and knowledge of the One. They are covered from reality, by the ignorance and denial of man's spiritual heritage.

Human beings always seek approval of what they do whether evil or good. We seek outer and inner confirmation. The self is like a mirror that seeks certainty of the image it reflects. The unbelievers are in despair due to their lack of reliance and contentment with divine decrees and perfect signs.

When a wayward person attains some outer success, due to Allah's generosity, he may be heading for greater shock or grief when it comes to an end or when circumstances are reversed.

Selfish and Wrong actions are veils of the self; they are barriers to entry into the Creator's abode of perfect presence. In truth, all actions and attributes emanate from Him alone.

All the real prophets and messengers transmitted the same marvelous news to their people: nothing exists unless it is within the Creator's will and design. His control and knowledge are absolute. This is the original tablet of His will and whoever reads it well will be liberated from transitory shadows and falsehood.

5.

وَلَا يَحْسَبَنَّ الَّذِينَ كَفَرُوا أَنَّمَا نُمْلِي لَهُمْ خَيْرٌ لِأَنْفُسِهِمْ إِنَّمَا نُمْلِي لَهُمْ لِيَزْدَادُوا إِثْمًا وَلَهُمْ عَذَابٌ مُهِينٌ

Let not those who are in denial imagine that Our granting respite to them is good for them. We only grant them respite so they will increase in their wrong deeds, and for them is a humiliating punishment.

3/178

6.

لَا تَحْسَبَنَّ الَّذِينَ كَفَرُوا مُعْجِزِينَ فِي الْأَرْضِ وَمَأْوَاهُمُ النَّارُ وَلَبِئْسَ الْمَصِيرُ

Do not think that those who are in denial are able to find escape in the earth. Their abode will be the fire, a hopeless end.

24/57

7.

إِنَّ الَّذِينَ لَا يُؤْمِنُونَ بِآيَاتِ اللَّهِ لَا يَهْدِيهِمُ اللَّهُ وَلَهُمْ عَذَابٌ أَلِيمٌ

Surely, those who do not believe in Allah's signs will not be guided by Allah, and they will have a painful punishment.

16/104

8.

لَمْ يَكُنِ الَّذِينَ كَفَرُوا مِنْ أَهْلِ الْكِتَابِ وَالْمُشْرِكِينَ مُنْفَكِّينَ حَتَّى تَأْتِيَهُمُ الْبَيِّنَةُ رَسُولٌ مِنَ اللَّهِ يَتْلُو صُحُفًا مُطَهَّرَةً فِيهَا كُتُبٌ قَيِّمَةٌ وَمَا تَفَرَّقَ الَّذِينَ أُوتُوا الْكِتَابَ إِلَّا مِنْ بَعْدِ مَا جَاءَتْهُمُ الْبَيِّنَةُ

The people of the Book who are unbelievers and the pagans would not mend their ways until the clear sign came to them: A Messenger of Allah reciting a purified text, containing correct scriptures. Those who were given the Book did not divide into sects until after the clear sign came to them.

98/1-4

9.

وَإِذَا ذُكِّرُوا لَا يَذْكُرُونَ

When they are reminded, they do not heed.

37/13

10.

وَلَمَّا جَاءَهُمْ كِتَابٌ مِّنْ عِندِ اللَّهِ مُصَدِّقٌ لِّمَا مَعَهُمْ وَكَانُوا مِن قَبْلُ يَسْتَفْتِحُونَ عَلَى الَّذِينَ كَفَرُوا فَلَمَّا جَاءَهُم مَّا عَرَفُوا كَفَرُوا بِهِ فَلَعْنَةُ اللَّهِ عَلَى الْكَافِرِينَ

When a book comes to them from Allah, confirming what is with them, even though before that they used to invoke Allah for victory over those who disbelieve, and when what they recognise has come to them, they denied it. Allah's curse is on the unbelievers.

2/89

11.

وَلَوْ شِئْنَا لَرَفَعْنَاهُ بِهَا وَلَٰكِنَّهُ أَخْلَدَ إِلَى الْأَرْضِ وَاتَّبَعَ هَوَاهُ فَمَثَلُهُ كَمَثَلِ الْكَلْبِ إِن تَحْمِلْ عَلَيْهِ يَلْهَثْ أَوْ تَتْرُكْهُ يَلْهَث ذَّٰلِكَ مَثَلُ الْقَوْمِ الَّذِينَ كَذَّبُوا بِآيَاتِنَا فَاقْصُصِ الْقَصَصَ لَعَلَّهُمْ يَتَفَكَّرُونَ

If We had willed, We would have raised him up thereby, but he clung to the earth and pursued his own whims and base desires. Therefore, he is likened to a dog: you chase it away, it lolls its tongue out and pants, and if you leave it alone it does the same (nothing changes its behaviour). This is the likeness of those who deny Our signs. Relate the narrative so hopefully they will reflect.

7/176

His books are made up of His words. His commands emanate from Him through multiple streams of light of different qualities and designations. They bring about his creational designs and patterns.

This world is a transit station and prelude for the Hereafter. Its purpose is for the human self to realize its spiritual reality and live by it. The unbeliever is the unfortunate being who denies this gift and is imprisoned by the ego, which is only a shadow of the everlasting soul.

Departure from this life and arrival in the next experience will be smooth and joyful for those who are prepared for arrival and departure.

The ways of unbelief and denial, for the most part, are based on habits of society and cultural traditions. This temporary ease of familiarity and solace can only lead to a disastrous shock when the truth regarding the true nature of life and the source of existence is revealed.

If we are not awakened to awareness of Him then we remain blind and sick at heart. No healing or 'forgiveness' can take place unless we are ready to leave falsehood.

12.

يَـٰبَنِىٓ إِسۡرَٰٓءِيلَ ٱذۡكُرُواْ نِعۡمَتِىَ ٱلَّتِىٓ أَنۡعَمۡتُ عَلَيۡكُمۡ وَأَنِّى فَضَّلۡتُكُمۡ عَلَى ٱلۡعَٰلَمِينَ

O tribe of Israel, remember the blessing I conferred upon you, and that I favoured you over all other beings.

2/122

13.

لَا يَغُرَّنَّكَ تَقَلُّبُ ٱلَّذِينَ كَفَرُواْ فِى ٱلۡبِلَٰدِ مَتَٰعٌ قَلِيلٌ ثُمَّ مَأۡوَىٰهُمۡ جَهَنَّمُ وَبِئۡسَ ٱلۡمِهَادُ

Do not be deceived that those who are in denial move freely about the earth. It is but a brief enjoyment, and then their abode will be hell-fire. Therein is an evil resting-place

3/196-197

14.

فَلَوۡلَآ إِذۡ جَآءَهُم بَأۡسُنَا تَضَرَّعُواْ وَلَٰكِن قَسَتۡ قُلُوبُهُمۡ وَزَيَّنَ لَهُمُ ٱلشَّيۡطَٰنُ مَا كَانُواْ يَعۡمَلُونَ

If only they had humbled themselves when Our violent force came upon them! However, their hearts were hard, and *Shaytān* made what they were doing seem attractive to them.

6/43

15.

وَإِذَا قِيلَ لَهُمُ ٱتَّبِعُواْ مَآ أَنزَلَ ٱللَّهُ قَالُواْ بَلۡ نَتَّبِعُ مَآ أَلۡفَيۡنَا عَلَيۡهِ ءَابَآءَنَآ أَوَلَوۡ كَانَ ءَابَآؤُهُمۡ لَا يَعۡقِلُونَ شَيۡـًٔا وَلَا يَهۡتَدُونَ

And when it is said to them: follow what Allah has revealed. They say: But surely we must follow that which our fathers followed. Even though their fathers had no intellect and were not guided

2/170

16.

وَمَنْ أَعْرَضَ عَن ذِكْرِي فَإِنَّ لَهُ مَعِيشَةً ضَنكًا وَنَحْشُرُهُ يَوْمَ الْقِيَامَةِ أَعْمَىٰ

Whoever turns away from My remembrance, will live a restricted life, and on the Day of Rising We will bring him forth blind

20/124

17.

سَوَاءٌ عَلَيْهِمْ أَسْتَغْفَرْتَ لَهُمْ أَمْ لَمْ تَسْتَغْفِرْ لَهُمْ لَن يَغْفِرَ اللَّهُ لَهُمْ إِنَّ اللَّهَ لَا يَهْدِي الْقَوْمَ الْفَاسِقِينَ

It is the same to them whether you ask forgiveness for them or not ask forgiveness for them. Allah will never forgive them. Allah does not guide those who deviate from the right way.

63/6

18.

وَقَدْ نَزَّلَ عَلَيْكُمْ فِي الْكِتَابِ أَنْ إِذَا سَمِعْتُمْ آيَاتِ اللَّهِ يُكْفَرُ بِهَا وَيُسْتَهْزَأُ بِهَا فَلَا تَقْعُدُوا مَعَهُمْ حَتَّىٰ يَخُوضُوا فِي حَدِيثٍ غَيْرِهِ إِنَّكُمْ إِذًا مِّثْلُهُمْ إِنَّ اللَّهَ جَامِعُ الْمُنَافِقِينَ وَالْكَافِرِينَ فِي جَهَنَّمَ جَمِيعًا

It has been sent down to you in the Book that when you hear Allah's signs being rejected and mocked by people, you must not sit with them until they start talking of other things. If you do not, you are just the same as they are. Allah will gather all the hypocrites and unbelievers together in hell.

4/140

Allah's messages and signs flow continuously as part of His ongoing mercy. His ways are both powerful and subtle. They always prevail. Often we are caught in the events and do not read the message and meaning behind them. We usually deal with the outer symptoms of an illness without looking for its root cause, which is always due to deviation from a balanced and perfect lifestyle.

Without reflection we cover up the truth and follow our superficial habits, whimsical desires and futile pleasures. Preoccupation with the self is the state of those at a loss.

The security we seek in this world is as flimsy as a spider's web. Caring for one's self is a natural positive force in everyone, but the wish for prolonged life and fear of death are clear signs of stunted spiritual growth. In truth, life is eternal. The Hereafter is but a different timeless phase of existence.

When the self is subservient to the soul it is ready to leave this world anytime. All love and passion is for and by the Creator and His world of time and space. To witness the Beloved Possessor of perfect beauty and majesty at all times and yearning to be with Him is the state of the passionate seeking for Truth.

The unbelievers are trapped in their darkness and confusion. They reflect the worst of deep ignorance and injustice in creation.

19.

وَإِذْ يَمْكُرُ بِكَ الَّذِينَ كَفَرُوا لِيُثْبِتُوكَ أَوْ يَقْتُلُوكَ أَوْ يُخْرِجُوكَ وَيَمْكُرُونَ وَيَمْكُرُ اللَّهُ وَاللَّهُ خَيْرُ الْمَاكِرِينَ

When those who are in denial were plotting against you to imprison, kill, or expel you, they were planning, and Allah was planning; but Allah is the best of planners.

8/30

20.

إِنَّهُمْ يَكِيدُونَ كَيْدًا
وَأَكِيدُ كَيْدًا
فَمَهِّلِ الْكَافِرِينَ أَمْهِلْهُمْ رُوَيْدًا

Surely they scheme, and I set forth My plan. So bear with the unbelievers for a while.

86/15-17

21.

مَثَلُ الَّذِينَ اتَّخَذُوا مِنْ دُونِ اللَّهِ أَوْلِيَاءَ كَمَثَلِ الْعَنْكَبُوتِ اتَّخَذَتْ بَيْتًا وَإِنَّ أَوْهَنَ الْبُيُوتِ لَبَيْتُ الْعَنْكَبُوتِ لَوْ كَانُوا يَعْلَمُونَ

The likeness of those who take protectors besides Allah is like that of a spider that makes for itself a house. Surely, no house is flimsier than a spider's house. If only they knew.

29/41

22.

قُلْ إِنْ كَانَتْ لَكُمُ الدَّارُ الْآخِرَةُ عِنْدَ اللَّهِ خَالِصَةً مِنْ دُونِ النَّاسِ فَتَمَنَّوُا الْمَوْتَ إِنْ كُنْتُمْ صَادِقِينَ
وَلَنْ يَتَمَنَّوْهُ أَبَدًا بِمَا قَدَّمَتْ أَيْدِيهِمْ وَاللَّهُ عَلِيمٌ بِالظَّالِمِينَ

Say: If the abode of the Hereafter with Allah is for you alone, to the exclusion of others, then long for death if you are truthful. But they will never long for it because of what they have done. Allah knows the wrongdoers.

2/94-95

23.

وَالَّذِينَ كَذَّبُوا بِآيَاتِنَا سَنَسْتَدْرِجُهُم مِّنْ حَيْثُ لَا يَعْلَمُونَ
وَأُمْلِي لَهُمْ إِنَّ كَيْدِي مَتِينٌ

Those who deny Our Signs We lead step by step and they don't recognize. I grant them plenty of respite. Surely my plan is unassailable.

7/182-183

24.

فَلَا تُطِعِ الْكَافِرِينَ وَجَاهِدْهُم بِهِ جِهَادًا كَبِيرًا

Do not obey the unbelievers, and struggle against them with a firm resolve.

25/52

25.

لِّيُعَذِّبَ اللَّهُ الْمُنَافِقِينَ وَالْمُنَافِقَاتِ وَالْمُشْرِكِينَ وَالْمُشْرِكَاتِ وَيَتُوبَ اللَّهُ عَلَى الْمُؤْمِنِينَ وَالْمُؤْمِنَاتِ وَكَانَ اللَّهُ غَفُورًا رَّحِيمًا

Allah will punish the hypocrites, both men and women, as well as men and women who associate partners with Allah, and Allah will pardon men and women of faith. Allah is Forgiving, Merciful

33/73

26.

قَالَتِ الْأَعْرَابُ آمَنَّا قُل لَّمْ تُؤْمِنُوا وَلَٰكِن قُولُوا أَسْلَمْنَا وَلَمَّا يَدْخُلِ الْإِيمَانُ فِي قُلُوبِكُمْ وَإِن تُطِيعُوا اللَّهَ وَرَسُولَهُ لَا يَلِتْكُم مِّنْ أَعْمَالِكُمْ شَيْئًا إِنَّ اللَّهَ غَفُورٌ رَّحِيمٌ

The (desert) Arabs say: We believe. Say: You do not believe. Rather say: We submit, for faith has not yet entered your hearts. And if you obey Allah and His messenger He will not diminish anything of your deeds. Certainly, Allah is Forgiving, Merciful.

49/14

The unbelievers are trapped in their darkness and confusion. They reflect the worst of deep ignorance and injustice in creation, thus afflicting other weak human beings with their contagious sickness of hypocrisy and barren reasoning. Rationality and reason are necessary steps to reach the ocean of spiritual bliss. However, without unswerving devotion and utter surrender, one remains on the barren shore.

The desert Arabs are described as the most hypocritical, treacherous and rebellious people. These qualities have increased even more with the passage of time and with further deviation from the path of enlightenment.

Weak-minded beings do not realize the purpose of this life and thus are not prepared for the Hereafter. Wise is the one who lives in this world prepared for the final departure. Otherwise, the end will be a shocking, grievous affair.

Constant awareness and responsible accountability reduces the risk of corruption of the soul and transgression.

27.

الْأَعْرَابُ أَشَدُّ كُفْرًا وَنِفَاقًا وَأَجْدَرُ أَلَّا يَعْلَمُوا حُدُودَ مَا أَنزَلَ اللَّهُ عَلَىٰ رَسُولِهِ وَاللَّهُ عَلِيمٌ حَكِيمٌ

The (desert) Arabs are capable of the worst denial and hypocrisy, and more likely to be ignorant of the limits, which Allah has revealed to His messenger. But Allah is Knowing, Wise.

9/97

28.

لَقَدْ كَفَرَ الَّذِينَ قَالُوا إِنَّ اللَّهَ ثَالِثُ ثَلَاثَةٍ وَمَا مِنْ إِلَٰهٍ إِلَّا إِلَٰهٌ وَاحِدٌ وَإِن لَّمْ يَنتَهُوا عَمَّا يَقُولُونَ لَيَمَسَّنَّ الَّذِينَ كَفَرُوا مِنْهُمْ عَذَابٌ أَلِيمٌ

Surely, those who say Allah is the third of three are disbelievers. There is no God except one God. And if they do not desist from what they say, a painful doom will certainly fall on those who reject faith.

5/73

29

إِنَّهُمْ كَانُوا لَا يَرْجُونَ حِسَابًا
وَكَذَّبُوا بِآيَاتِنَا كِذَّابًا
وَكُلَّ شَيْءٍ أَحْصَيْنَاهُ كِتَابًا
فَذُوقُوا فَلَن نَّزِيدَكُمْ إِلَّا عَذَابًا

Indeed, they did not expect to have a reckoning, and they utterly denied Our signs. But everything has been recorded in a Book. So taste (what you earned), and We shall not increase you except in punishment.

78/27-30

30.

وَلِلَّذِينَ كَفَرُوا بِرَبِّهِمْ عَذَابُ جَهَنَّمَ وَبِئْسَ الْمَصِيرُ

For those who deny their Lord, there is the punishment of hell. What an evil destination.

67/6

CHAPTER THIRTEEN

THE HEREAFTER

The continuation of life after death is the cornerstone of all prophetic teachings. The Qur'an brings this creational issue to the fore. Indeed, Islam is built on the foundation of awareness and remembrance and reference to the Hereafter. In terms of human conduct, self-awareness and remembrance of death - accountability for one's actions is a major factor in self-correction and illumination.

Allah describes the condition of the Hereafter as based on the individual's experience of past actions and intentions in this world. Each person will experience and relive what they have earned in this life. All worldly attempts to bring about justice are echoes of absolute Divine Justice. Paradise and hell are the two extremes, states or destinies, which an individual will experience as a consequence of their worldly journey. Those who are perpetuating brutality and tyranny without accountability will be requited for their wrongdoing in the next phase. Those who have lived in piety and service, maintaining peace and contentment, will enter the abode of permanent bliss in the garden of the Hereafter.

This world, caught in time and space, is the realm of relative experience that leads to a boundless phase beyond it. Adam was created in the garden before the distinction between it and hell was made. His children have to earn their return to that garden through intelligent submission and dedicated action.

The pleasures and afflictions of this world are only small samples of the everlasting experience of the Hereafter. Thus there are many minor hells and gardens in this world. We shall experience in that realm what we have earned here. If we have come to realize the One Divine Light behind all light and shadows in this world, then after departure from this body that knowledge will deliver the self to its appropriate new phase.

1.

إِذَا زُلْزِلَتِ الْأَرْضُ زِلْزَالَهَا
وَأَخْرَجَتِ الْأَرْضُ أَثْقَالَهَا
وَقَالَ الْإِنسَانُ مَالَهَا
يَوْمَئِذٍ تُحَدِّثُ أَخْبَارَهَا
بِأَنَّ رَبَّكَ أَوْحَىٰ لَهَا
يَوْمَئِذٍ يَصْدُرُ النَّاسُ أَشْتَاتًا لِّيُرَوْا أَعْمَالَهُمْ
فَمَن يَعْمَلْ مِثْقَالَ ذَرَّةٍ خَيْرًا يَرَهُ
وَمَن يَعْمَلْ مِثْقَالَ ذَرَّةٍ شَرًّا يَرَهُ

When the Earth is violently convulsed, and brings forth her burdens, man will say: What is the matter with her? That day she will relate all her stored chronicles, because your Lord has inspired her. That day people will come forth in groups to be shown their deeds. Whoever does an atom's weight of good will see it, and whoever does an atom's weight of evil will see it.

99/1-8

The physical universe will one day end as it began, and all human souls will experience another phase of life whose quality will be according to the extent of their spiritual awakening and enlightenment. Our experiences in the temporary abode of time and space will ultimately lead to the zone of timelessness – the eternal Hereafter.

2.

إِذَا السَّمَاءُ انفَطَرَتْ
وَإِذَا الْكَوَاكِبُ انتَثَرَتْ
وَإِذَا الْبِحَارُ فُجِّرَتْ
وَإِذَا الْقُبُورُ بُعْثِرَتْ
عَلِمَتْ نَفْسٌ مَّا قَدَّمَتْ وَأَخَّرَتْ
يَا أَيُّهَا الْإِنسَانُ مَا غَرَّكَ بِرَبِّكَ الْكَرِيمِ
الَّذِي خَلَقَكَ فَسَوَّاكَ فَعَدَلَكَ
فِي أَيِّ صُورَةٍ مَّا شَاءَ رَكَّبَكَ

When the heaven is split apart, And the heavenly bodies are strewn about, when the seas pour forth, and the graves are overturned, every soul will know what it has sent before it and what it has left behind. O mankind, what has made you careless concerning your Lord, the Bountiful, Who created you, and fashioned you proportionately, in whatever form He desired to insert you in.

82/1-8

The seeds for submission to Allah and obedience to Him are sown in this world. The harvest will be reaped in the next phase of existence where human action is not possible.

The ultimate event of the Day of Reckoning is described as the final, global shattering and disintegration. The entire universe will revert to its original, singular wholeness.

When this existence ends, creation will witness the One source and truth behind all previous experiences and will relive past actions and states. The account in the Hereafter is rendered according to these actions. The self will be judged and rewarded by the One Lord according to its extent of knowledge and enlightenment.

The Day of Reckoning is when all apparent dispersions end, and the infinite varieties of creations experience the divine gatheredness.

3.

إِذَا وَقَعَتِ ٱلْوَاقِعَةُ
لَيْسَ لِوَقْعَتِهَا كَاذِبَةٌ
خَافِضَةٌ رَّافِعَةٌ
إِذَا رُجَّتِ ٱلْأَرْضُ رَجًّا

When the event occurs, there is no denying that it will occur, abasing (some), exalting (others); when the earth is shaken with a shock.

56/1-4

4.

إِذَا ٱلسَّمَاءُ ٱنشَقَّتْ
وَأَذِنَتْ لِرَبِّهَا وَحُقَّتْ
وَإِذَا ٱلْأَرْضُ مُدَّتْ
وَأَلْقَتْ مَا فِيهَا وَتَخَلَّتْ
وَأَذِنَتْ لِرَبِّهَا وَحُقَّتْ
يَٰٓأَيُّهَا ٱلْإِنسَٰنُ إِنَّكَ كَادِحٌ إِلَىٰ رَبِّكَ كَدْحًا فَمُلَٰقِيهِ
فَأَمَّا مَنْ أُوتِىَ كِتَٰبَهُۥ بِيَمِينِهِۦ
فَسَوْفَ يُحَاسَبُ حِسَابًا يَسِيرًا
وَيَنقَلِبُ إِلَىٰٓ أَهْلِهِۦ مَسْرُورًا
وَأَمَّا مَنْ أُوتِىَ كِتَٰبَهُۥ وَرَآءَ ظَهْرِهِۦ
فَسَوْفَ يَدْعُواْ ثُبُورًا

When the heaven is split open. And is attentive to it's Lord as it must be. When the earth is spread out. And has cast out all that was within her and is empty, obeying it's Lord as it must do. O mankind, you are toiling to your Lord with your deeds and actions, striving, and you certainly will meet Him. Then whoever is given his account in his right hand; He truly will receive an easy reckoning. And will return to his people in joy. But whoever is given his account behind his back, he surely will invoke destruction.

84/1-11

The Hereafter

In that phase, there is no veil over the ultimate truth, and everything will be clearly seen for what it is. When His Unique Light is unveiled, there are no shadows.

5.

لَا أُقْسِمُ بِيَوْمِ ٱلْقِيَامَةِ ۝ وَلَا أُقْسِمُ بِٱلنَّفْسِ ٱللَّوَّامَةِ ۝ أَيَحْسَبُ ٱلْإِنسَٰنُ أَلَّن نَجْمَعَ عِظَامَهُۥ ۝ بَلَىٰ قَٰدِرِينَ عَلَىٰٓ أَن نُّسَوِّىَ بَنَانَهُۥ ۝ بَلْ يُرِيدُ ٱلْإِنسَٰنُ لِيَفْجُرَ أَمَامَهُۥ ۝ يَسْـَٔلُ أَيَّانَ يَوْمُ ٱلْقِيَامَةِ ۝ فَإِذَا بَرِقَ ٱلْبَصَرُ ۝ وَخَسَفَ ٱلْقَمَرُ ۝ وَجُمِعَ ٱلشَّمْسُ وَٱلْقَمَرُ ۝ يَقُولُ ٱلْإِنسَٰنُ يَوْمَئِذٍ أَيْنَ ٱلْمَفَرُّ ۝ كَلَّا لَا وَزَرَ ۝ إِلَىٰ رَبِّكَ يَوْمَئِذٍ ٱلْمُسْتَقَرُّ ۝ يُنَبَّؤُا۟ ٱلْإِنسَٰنُ يَوْمَئِذٍۭ بِمَا قَدَّمَ وَأَخَّرَ ۝ بَلِ ٱلْإِنسَٰنُ عَلَىٰ نَفْسِهِۦ بَصِيرَةٌ ۝ وَلَوْ أَلْقَىٰ مَعَاذِيرَهُۥ ۝

I swear by the Day of Resurrection, and I swear by the blaming self. Does man think that We shall not reassemble his bones? Certainly, We are able to restore his very fingers! Yet man would still deny what is before him, asking: When is this Day of Resurrection? When sight is dazzled, and the moon is eclipsed, and the sun and the moon are united, on that day man will cry: Where can I flee? Alas, there is no refuge. On that day the only resting place will be with your Lord. On that day man is told the tale of that which he has sent before and left behind. Oh, but man is a telling witness against himself, although he puts forth his excuses

75/1-15

On that day, each being will see the reality of their past life and the extent of their distractions and ignorance of the Lord. On the day of reckoning the soul and self will unite with the physical and will be fully exposed to the One source of Light.

6.

ٱقْتَرَبَ لِلنَّاسِ حِسَابُهُمْ وَهُمْ فِى غَفْلَةٍ مُّعْرِضُونَ

Mankind's reckoning has drawn close, yet they heedlessly turn away.

21/1

The same way that individuals will see their true reality, so will groups of people and nations.

Indeed, for the serious seeker, every day is a reminder of the last day.

The vigilant seeker remembers death and the next life constantly. This remembrance brings about heightened awareness and responsibility. With such focused discipline, the seeker is in constant anticipation of the Day of Reckoning, and every moment is deep and telling.

Good actions multiply, and evil actions cause equivalent afflictions. His justice and generosity are supreme in time and beyond time.

7.

وَيَوْمَ تَقُومُ السَّاعَةُ يَوْمَئِذٍ يَخْسَرُ الْمُبْطِلُونَ
وَتَرَىٰ كُلَّ أُمَّةٍ جَاثِيَةً كُلُّ أُمَّةٍ تُدْعَىٰ إِلَىٰ كِتَابِهَا
الْيَوْمَ تُجْزَوْنَ مَا كُنتُمْ تَعْمَلُونَ

…On the day when the Hour arises, on that day those who follow falsehood will be lost. You will see every nation on its knees, each nation summoned to its record. Today you will be repaid for what you did.

45/27-28

8.

إِنَّهُمْ يَرَوْنَهُ بَعِيدًا
وَنَرَاهُ قَرِيبًا

Behold, they see it far away. While we see it very close.

70/6-7

9.

إِنَّ السَّاعَةَ آتِيَةٌ أَكَادُ أُخْفِيهَا لِتُجْزَىٰ كُلُّ نَفْسٍ بِمَا تَسْعَىٰ

Behold, the Hour is coming. I have kept it seemingly hidden, so that every soul may be rewarded for that which it strives.

20/15

10.

مَن جَاءَ بِالْحَسَنَةِ فَلَهُ خَيْرٌ مِّنْهَا وَهُم مِّن فَزَعٍ
يَوْمَئِذٍ آمِنُونَ
وَمَن جَاءَ بِالسَّيِّئَةِ فَكُبَّتْ وُجُوهُهُمْ فِي النَّارِ هَلْ
تُجْزَوْنَ إِلَّا مَا كُنتُمْ تَعْمَلُونَ

Whoever brings a good deed will have better than it's worth, and they are safe from fear that day. And whoever brings an evil deed will be cast down on their faces in the Fire. Are you being repaid for anything other than what you did?

27/89-90

11.

وَوُضِعَ الْكِتَابُ فَتَرَى الْمُجْرِمِينَ مُشْفِقِينَ مِمَّا فِيهِ وَيَقُولُونَ يَا وَيْلَتَنَا مَالِ هَٰذَا الْكِتَابِ لَا يُغَادِرُ صَغِيرَةً وَلَا كَبِيرَةً إِلَّا أَحْصَاهَا وَوَجَدُوا مَا عَمِلُوا حَاضِرًا وَلَا يَظْلِمُ رَبُّكَ أَحَدًا

The Book will be set in place and you will see the guilty fearful of what is in it. They will say: Woe be to us, this book leaves out no action great or small without recording it. They will find everything they did present, and your Lord will wrong no one.
18/49

12.

وَكُلَّ إِنسَانٍ أَلْزَمْنَاهُ طَائِرَهُ فِي عُنُقِهِ وَنُخْرِجُ لَهُ يَوْمَ الْقِيَامَةِ كِتَابًا يَلْقَاهُ مَنشُورًا

We have fastened every man's destiny to his neck. On the Day of Reckoning We shall bring forth for him a book, spread wide open.
17/13

13.

أَلَمْ تَكُنْ آيَاتِي تُتْلَىٰ عَلَيْكُمْ فَكُنتُم بِهَا تُكَذِّبُونَ قَالُوا رَبَّنَا غَلَبَتْ عَلَيْنَا شِقْوَتُنَا وَكُنَّا قَوْمًا ضَالِّينَ

Were not My signs shown to you but you considered then false? They will say, "Our hard, Our misfortune has overcome us and we have become a people astray".
23/105-106

A person's 'book' is what he is writing in this world by his actions and intentions. We are the authors of our final destiny. This personal inner book is within our bodies, minds and hearts.

Everything we think, intend or act upon has an effect that is registered within our memories and physical cells. This truth will be fully revealed on the day of Reckoning, when all veils and barriers are removed.

His mercy is constantly witnessed through His signs and unveilings, yet, most people don't heed.

Time and space are relative phenomena. When you recall past years, they appear as a passing flash. In the same way, the human soul recalls the years of life on earth as a day or a few hours only. For the Lord of Creation, one day is the equivalent of a thousand years that human beings count.

Death is only the gateway of leaving one transient phase of existence to enter upon another that has no boundaries of time and space. Death is the threshold between the two modes of life.

The swiftest ascent to the gardens of the Hereafter is by a wholesome and pure heart, avoidance of distraction and unconditional love and obedience to Allah. The steed of ascent is energised by knowledge of Him and His glorious qualities.

Whatever we have done in this life will be found present there and experienced accordingly.

14.

وَيَوْمَ تَقُومُ ٱلسَّاعَةُ يُقْسِمُ ٱلْمُجْرِمُونَ مَا لَبِثُوا غَيْرَ سَاعَةٍ كَذَٰلِكَ كَانُوا يُؤْفَكُونَ

On that day, when the Hour arises, the guilty will swear that they did not remain but an hour. This is how they were deceived.

30/55

15.

قَالَ كَمْ لَبِثْتُمْ فِي ٱلْأَرْضِ عَدَدَ سِنِينَ
قَالُوا لَبِثْنَا يَوْمًا أَوْ بَعْضَ يَوْمٍ فَاسْأَلِ ٱلْعَادِّينَ
قَالَ إِن لَّبِثْتُمْ إِلَّا قَلِيلًا لَّوْ أَنَّكُمْ كُنتُمْ تَعْلَمُونَ

He will say: How many years did you remain on Earth? They will say: We stayed but a day or part of a day. So ask those who keep count. He will say: You stayed only a little while if you had only known.

23/112-114

16.

وَجَاءَتْ سَكْرَةُ ٱلْمَوْتِ بِٱلْحَقِّ ذَٰلِكَ مَا كُنتَ مِنْهُ تَحِيدُ
وَنُفِخَ فِي ٱلصُّورِ ذَٰلِكَ يَوْمُ ٱلْوَعِيدِ
وَجَاءَتْ كُلُّ نَفْسٍ مَّعَهَا سَائِقٌ وَشَهِيدٌ

The throes of death come revealing the truth, which is what you were trying to evade. And the trumpet is blown. This is the appointed day. Every soul comes with a driver and a witness.

50/19-21

17.

إِلَّا مَنْ أَتَى ٱللَّهَ بِقَلْبٍ سَلِيمٍ

Except one who comes to Allah with a wholesome heart.

89/26

18.

وَبَشِّرِ الَّذِينَ آمَنُوا وَعَمِلُوا الصَّالِحَاتِ أَنَّ لَهُمْ جَنَّاتٍ تَجْرِي مِن تَحْتِهَا الْأَنْهَارُ ۖ كُلَّمَا رُزِقُوا مِنْهَا مِن ثَمَرَةٍ رِّزْقًا ۙ قَالُوا هَٰذَا الَّذِي رُزِقْنَا مِن قَبْلُ ۖ وَأُتُوا بِهِ مُتَشَابِهًا ۖ وَلَهُمْ فِيهَا أَزْوَاجٌ مُّطَهَّرَةٌ ۖ وَهُمْ فِيهَا خَالِدُونَ

Give glad tidings to those who believe and do good works that theirs are gardens underneath which rivers flow. Every time they are provided with fruits from therein they say: This is what we were given before, and a resemblance is given to them. In it are pure companions for them, and they shall abide in it forever

2/25

19.

يَا أَيُّهَا الَّذِينَ آمَنُوا تُوبُوا إِلَى اللَّهِ تَوْبَةً نَّصُوحًا عَسَىٰ رَبُّكُمْ أَن يُكَفِّرَ عَنكُمْ سَيِّئَاتِكُمْ وَيُدْخِلَكُمْ جَنَّاتٍ تَجْرِي مِن تَحْتِهَا الْأَنْهَارُ يَوْمَ لَا يُخْزِي اللَّهُ النَّبِيَّ وَالَّذِينَ آمَنُوا مَعَهُ ۖ نُورُهُمْ يَسْعَىٰ بَيْنَ أَيْدِيهِمْ وَبِأَيْمَانِهِمْ يَقُولُونَ رَبَّنَا أَتْمِمْ لَنَا نُورَنَا وَاغْفِرْ لَنَا ۖ إِنَّكَ عَلَىٰ كُلِّ شَيْءٍ قَدِيرٌ

O You who believe, turn to Allah in sincere repentance. It may be that your Lord will remit your evil deeds and bring you into gardens underneath which rivers flow. On that day Allah will not degrade the Prophet and those who believe with him. Their light will run before them and on their right hands. They will say: Our Lord, perfect our light for us, and forgive us. Indeed, you are able to do all things.

66/8

20.

وَأُزْلِفَتِ الْجَنَّةُ لِلْمُتَّقِينَ غَيْرَ بَعِيدٍ ۝ هَٰذَا مَا تُوعَدُونَ لِكُلِّ أَوَّابٍ حَفِيظٍ ۝ مَّنْ خَشِيَ الرَّحْمَٰنَ بِالْغَيْبِ وَجَاءَ بِقَلْبٍ مُّنِيبٍ ۝ ادْخُلُوهَا بِسَلَامٍ ۖ ذَٰلِكَ يَوْمُ الْخُلُودِ

The garden is brought close for the truly aware, no longer distant. This is what you were promised, for every one who turns (to Allah) and protects (his faith). Who fears the Beneficent in the unseen and comes with a penitent heart.

50/31-34

Invisible rivers nourish the eternal gardens. No needs or desires arise there - pure bliss forever. This is the abode of trusting seekers whose hearts are pure and thus overflow with divine light.

The dwellers of the garden are those who arrive with a penitent heart full of caution and hope, overflowing with high expectations of Allah, the Most Generous and Merciful.

The hearts of the true servants and lovers of Allah experience the knowledge and closeness of the Eternal Garden in this world. They enter Eden with contended and peaceful hearts.

CONCLUSION

Human experience which is in the visible and discernible world is the gateway to the infinite unseen Reality. The Qur'an reveals the entire story of duality and the inseparability of self and soul as well as the limited and conditioned life on earth and the perpetual nature of life and consciousness. Our purpose in life is to read and live by Truth at all levels of manifestation. All human effort strives to be liberated from the illusion of space and time. This description, when used as a prescription may bring about transformation and unison between the human and divine.

To obtain these titles in ebook or hard copy, please visit
www.zahrapublications.com and www.sfhfoundation.com

General Books on Islam

Living Islam – East and West
Ageless and universal wisdom set against the backdrop of a changing world: application of this knowledge to one's own life is most appropriate.

The Elements of Islam/Thoughtful Guide to Islam
An introduction to Islam through an overview of the universality and light of the prophetic message.

The Qur'an & Its Teachings

Beams of Illumination from the Divine Revelations
A collection of teachings and talks with the objective of exploring deeper meanings of Qur'anic Revelations.

Commentary on Four Selected Chapters of the Qur'an
The Shaykh uncovers inner meanings, roots and subtleties of the Qur'anic Arabic terminology.

The Cow: Commentary on Chapters One and Two of the Holy Qur'an
The first two chapters of the Qur'an give guidance regarding inner and outer struggle. Emphasis is on understanding key Qur'anic terms.

The Family of `Imran
This book is a commentary on the third chapter of the Qur'an, the family of `Imran which includes the story of Mary, mother of `Isa (Jesus).

The Essential Message of the Qur'an
Teachings from the Qur'an such as purpose of creation, Attributes of the Creator, nature of human beings, decrees governing the laws of the universe, life and death.

Heart of Qur'an and Perfect Mizan
Commentary on chapter Yasin. This is traditionally read over the dead person: if we want to know the meaning of life, we have to learn about death.

Journey of the Universe as Expounded in the Qur'an
The Qur'an traces the journey of all creation, seeing the physical, biological and geological voyage of life as paralleled by the inner spiritual evolution of wo/man.

Qur'an's Prescription for Life
Understanding of the Qur'an is made accessible with easy reference to key issues concerning life, and the path of Islam.

The Story of Creation in the Qur'an – A Sufi Interpretation
An exposition of the Qur'anic verses relating to the nature of physical phenomena, including the origins of the universe, the nature of light, matter, space and time, and the evolution of biological and sentient beings.

Sufism & Islamic Psychology and Philosophy

Beginning's End
This is a contemporary outlook on Sufi sciences of self knowledge, exposing the challenge of our modern lifestyle that is out of balance.

Cosmology of the Self
Islamic teachings of Tawhid (Unity) with insights into the human self: understanding the inner landscape is essential foundation for progress on the path of knowledge.

The Elements of Sufism/Thoughtful Guide to Sufism
Sufism is the heart of Islam. This introduction describes its origins, practices, historical background and its spread throughout the world.

Happiness in Life and After Death – An Islamic Sufi View
This book offers revelations and spiritual teachings that map a basic path towards wholesome living without forgetting death: cultivating a constant awareness of one's dual nature.

The Journey of the Self

After introducing the basic model of the self, there follows a simple yet complete outline of the self's emergence, development, sustenance, and growth toward its highest potential.

Leaves from a Sufi Journal

A unique collection of articles presenting an outstanding introduction to the areas of Sufism and original Islamic teachings.

The Sufi Way to Self-Unfoldment

Unfolding inner meanings of the Islamic ritual practices towards the intended ultimate purpose to live a life honorable and fearless, with no darkness, ignorance or abuse.

Witnessing Perfection

Delves into the universal question of Deity and the purpose of life. Durable contentment is a result of 'perfected vision'.

Practices & Teachings of Islam

Calling Allah by His Most Beautiful Names

Attributes or Qualities resonate from their Majestic and Beautiful Higher Realm into the heart of the active seeker, and through it back into the world.

Fasting in Islam

This is a comprehensive guide to fasting in all its aspects, with a description of fasting in different faith traditions, its spiritual benefits, rules and regulations.

The Inner Meanings of Worship in Islam – A Personal Selection of Guidance for the Wayfarer

Here is guidance for those who journey along this path, from the Qur'an, the Prophet's traditions, narrations from the *Ahl al-Bayt*, and seminal works from among the *Ahl al-Tasawwuf* of all schools of thought.

Prophetic Traditions in Islam – On the Authority of the Family of the Prophet

Offers a comprehensive selection of Islamic teachings arranged according to topics dealing with belief and worship, moral, social and spiritual values.

The Wisdom (Hikam) of Ibn `Ata'allah – Translation and Commentary

These aphorisms of Ibn `Ata'Allah, a Shadhili Shaykh, reveal the breadth and depth of an enlightened being who reflects divine unity and inner transformation through worship.

The Sayings and Wisdom of Imām Ali

A selection of this great man's sayings gathered together from authentic and reliable sources. They have been carefully translated into modern English.

Transformative Worship in Islam: Experiencing Perfection

Uniquely bridges the traditional practices and beliefs, culture and language of Islam with the transformative spiritual states described by the Sufis and Gnostics.

The Lantern of the Path by Imam Ja'far al-Sadiq.

Imam Ja'far al-Sadiq was the founder of the Ja'fari School of Islamic Law and a renowned scholar of his age. The Imam shows in his ageless commentaries on the courtesies, practices and rituals of Islam the way to equilibrium in the most inspired and tawhidi way.

Talks & Courses

Ask Course 1 – The Sufi Map of the Self

This workbook explores the entire cosmology of the self through time, and maps the evolution of the self from before birth through life, death and beyond.

Ask Course 2 – The Prophetic Way of Life

This workbook explores how the code of ethics that govern religious practice and the Prophetic ways are in fact transformational tools to enlightened awakening.

Friday Discourses – Volume 1

The Shaykh addresses many topics that influence Muslims at the core of what it means to be a Muslim in today's global village.

Songs of Imān on the Roads of Pakistan

A series of talks given on the divergence between 'faith' and 'unbelief' during a tour of the country in 1982 which becomes a reflection of the condition occurring in the rest of the world today.

Poetry & Aphorisms

Sound Waves

A collection of aphorisms that help us reflect and discover the intricate connection between self and soul.

Beyond Windows

Offering moving and profound insights of compassion and spirituality through these anthologies of connections between slave self and Eternal Lord.

101 Helpful Illusions

Everything in creation has a purpose relevant to ultimate spiritual Truth. This book highlights natural veils to be transcended by disciplined courage, wisdom and insight.

Bursts of Silence

Inspired aphorisms provide keys to doors of inner knowledge, as well as antidotes to distraction and confusion.

Ripples of Light

Inspired aphorisms which become remedies for hearts that seek the truth.

Pointers to Presence

A collection of aphorisms providing insights into consciousness and are pointers to spiritual awakening.

Autobiography

Son of Karbala

The atmosphere of an Iraq in transition is brought to life and used as a backdrop for the Shaykh's own personal quest for self-discovery and spiritual truth.

To obtain these titles in ebook or hard copy, please visit
www.zahrapublications.com and www.sfhfoundation.com

www.ingramcontent.com/pod-product-compliance
Lightning Source LLC
Chambersburg PA
CBHW020858090426
42736CB00008B/413